ZEN DRIVING

K.T. Berger

Ballantine Books
New York

All rights reserved under International and
Pan-American Copyright Conventions.
Published in the United States by
Ballantine Books,
a division of Random House, Inc.,
New York, and simultaneously in Canada
by Random House of Canada Limited, Toronto.

Grateful acknowledgment is made to
Charles E. Tuttle Company, Inc., Tokyo, Japan,
for permission to reprint excerpts from
"The Gateless Gate" by Mumon in *Zen Flesh, Zen Bones*
by Paul Reps and Nyogen Senzaki.

Library of Congress Catalog Card Number: 87-91366

ISBN: 0-345-35350-1

Cover design by James R. Harris
Photo: FPG International/Dennis Hallinan
Book design by Alex Jay/Studio J

Manufactured in the United States of America

10 9 8 7

For our parents,
William and June Berger.

ZEN
DRIVING

CONTENTS

Special thanks
to our agent,
Robert Stricker,
and our editor
Chris Cox, and to
Christine Lazor.

ZEN
DRIVING

INTRODUCTION

*"So happy to see you,
I have nothing to say!"*

—*Zen Master Hakuin (1685–1768)*

Two ingredients go into creating a good driver: experience and awareness. This little book will give you neither. You cannot drive this book, therefore your experience will not increase; nor, without being behind the wheel, can you expect to expand your awareness. In fact, driving an automobile should be as natural as walking or running. It is folly to imagine that you can learn to become a good driver by reading a how-to book. This book, characteristically, will not *do* a thing. This book is an exercise in the Zen principle of "non-doing" or "non-action." There is no need for exertion as you travel along the words and pages that follow. It will not be necessary to master any seemingly abstruse Eastern philosophy. There is nothing to cling or attach to. This is the ease and beauty of such an approach. The way of Zen may be the most effective avenue to driving, but then driving itself is the best way to learn Zen. One is the application of the other. Ultimately, awareness and experience will be your only useful guides. The purpose of this book is to introduce you to those guides without getting in the way.

ONE

Friendly Persuasion: The Theory of Zen and Zen Driving

Buddha Behind the Wheel

The purpose of this book is to introduce you to pure awareness/experience, your *natural-self*, an innate ability waiting to unfold like a coiled snake. To take that unleashed energy, stick it in the ignition of your car, turn over the engine, put it in gear, and head off down the highway, practicing, in a merry state of mind, Zen Driving.

"But everybody already knows how to drive," a friend commented when I told her I was writing a book about Zen Driving. How, she wanted to know, was Zen Driving different from what she was doing? What could she expect to get out of practicing this Zen Driving? Especially, she added, since she was already "practicing" her *own* religion.

I explained that though Zen was a form of Buddhism it was separate from any religious doctrine. The Japanese word *Zen* literally means meditation, and meditation implies being fully aware, fully in touch with your surroundings. To be in a meditative state simply means to be in your natural-self, your Buddha Self. All very simple straightforward stuff. No religious flummery. In Zen, everyone has the Buddha Nature, everyone *is* (if only they would realize it!) the Buddha.

So what you want, I told her—just to cover all bases—is your plastic Jesus on the dash, and Buddha (yourself!) behind the wheel.

Opportunity Honking

As for the actual nitty-gritty benefits of Zen Driving, there are several. First, you will be a better driver. With an increased awareness of and a better feel for the car, the road, and yourself, you will move through traffic in a more fluid, efficient manner. As a result you will become a much *safer* driver. In other words, with awareness and ability at their peaks, you will not only *not* run into things—almost guaranteed—you will not *worry* about running into things.

All this ability and safety will pave the way for what I consider to be the major purpose of Zen Driving, and that is to thoroughly enjoy the driving experience. Driving can often be a dreaded, boring chore. Zen Driving eliminates those feelings. Driving in your car, ensconced in your own individual sacred space, is a golden opportunity to take time out from whatever you were previously doing, to turn off all worries, erase all mind chatter. And if you choose to use it this way, to be aware, to be on top of things, to feel hooked up and alive—well, a Buddha behind the wheel is a happy and contented driver.

Ultimately, your contented driving experience can spill over into other areas of your life. Those who practice yoga, meditation, and the martial arts all anticipate that not only will these practices make them feel better in the here-now, but that the centered here-now will segue into the rest of the day's activities. The nice thing about Zen Driving, unlike the above disciplines, happens to be that you *have* to drive. Zen Driving is a form of meditation/yoga everyone can do. The average American spends a minimum of one full hour a day in his or her car. You can exercise your mindfulness while you take yourself to work, to the store, to a movie. Who can deny that the time we spend in our cars—even if it's just a ten-minute trip to the local Safeway—does not affect our attitudes once back in the mad walking world? Wouldn't it be a joy if driving was actually a means of enhancing our destinations, not just, say, a tolerated chore, or a trial in anxiety?

The idea is to tap into an inner ability that allows you to feel good, so that when you arrive and park, like coming to the end of a ski run or a long meditation, you emerge in a fresher, more alive, more assured frame of mind. In short, and it may sound a bit corny or farfetched, you can improve the quality of your life through proper driving practice. Better living through better driving.

What is Zen Driving?

But what exactly *is* Zen Driving?

Well, now we come to a very difficult task right here at the start of things. Because to answer properly the question, "What is Zen Driving?" you yourself would have to *be* a Zen Driver *in* the process of Zen Driving. For a definition we cannot consult the Ancient Ones, the sutras, or oral tradition; nor do I believe there's an explanation in your local state driver's handbook. Zen Driving is an experienced state of being. Words don't do it much justice. To know exactly what it is you must experience it.

A young monk was sitting in his parked car next to the Great Highway. Riding shotgun was the Zen Master. The monk, eager and troubled, finally turned to the Master and pleaded, "Please, Zenji, show me the way to Zen Driving!" The Master replied, "Do you hear the rushing roar of the highway river next to us?" "Yes," the monk said, "I do." "Enter there," said the Master.

Enter There

You are now driving on the open country highway. No mind, no thought, no form. The shapely hills and orchards slip through your consciousness as gently as the warm wind. The white lines skate beneath you, the telephone poles and wires slide evenly by your side. Your hands on the steering wheel tingle with the rhythms of the whirring engine and you can feel your car around you as though you were wearing it. Floating through every turn, accelerating, passing slower vehicles, you can feel the road pouring under your tires. It's a glorious day and the sun is glistening; you, the road, and the car respond to every nuance of motion and traffic.

But now you are late for work in deep heavy downtown traffic. (Uh-oh.) Suddenly your Zen mind begins to wobble. Suddenly you're creeping along in the left lane, your hands already sweated to the wheel, when some fine fellow driving one of Detroit's finest (and largest) cuts you off. Deftness, natural agility, saves your insurance rates from going up. But that isn't what you experience. To you it's just pure dumb luck that saves you. Awareness gives way to suspicion. You grow uptight and overly cautious. You cinch your seat belt tighter. You ride the brakes. You recall the lousy thing your best friend said to you the other day—and nearly rear end the car in front of you! You slam your fist against the steering wheel. Junk! You want a new car. You want a new job. You start punching all the buttons on your car radio, but no song seems to fit this mood.

It sure would make a difference if driving in city traffic was as soothing and as enjoyable as driving on the open road. This is the song you're looking for. It's an inner tune. Real Zen Driving, when tuned in, allows you this unfettered feeling. With perfect aplomb you are able to respond to traffic situations instinctually. With unclouded confidence your awareness is keen, and maneuvering through traffic is like gliding along on a track. This is true Zen Driving, a self-assurance springing from a true sense of personal power and innate ability. But, unfortunately, this is not always your normal driving mode. (Perhaps it is *never* your normal driving mode!) It is something that must be developed. Furthermore, there exist impediments—personal *stuff*—that pop up to block and obfuscate this clear, natural driving ability. In reality, one minute you've got it, one minute you don't.

A Two–Pronged Approach

So, given this situation, how do you become a Zen Driver?

On one level you want to become aware—bring to your conscious attention—those impediments, often unconscious, that are blocking your natural abilities. According to Zen gospel, these impediments are caused by *delusions* and *attachments*. A student asked Roshi Kapleau, "What can a Zen teacher give me?" And Roshi Kapleau replied, "He can't give you anything you don't already have. But he can take away much that is foreign to your True-nature." It's not so much a matter of what's missing as it is a matter of what's getting in the way of what you already have.

The fact is, you already have the Buddha Nature, your natural-self. You already possess the innate ability to become a Zen Driver—if you would only realize (make real) the fact and use it. But, like having a million dollars, you can't spend it unless you remember which mattress you hid it under. Having it sit there, unaware, does you no good. The same is true with your natural-self, that which allows you to become a Zen Driver—you must realize you have it, constantly remember to use it, and simultaneously examine those things that cloud your remembering of it.

❁

I Do Have It (Don't I?)

In Zen, traditionally, this "it" has been difficult to elucidate. To begin with, it cannot be analyzed, isolated, or bought over the counter at your local drug store. It cannot be explained, it cannot be taught, it cannot be given or received. The reason being, as Zen claims, that there is nothing you need study or accomplish to have it, for you have had it from the day you were born. It is like the Zen story of a man riding on an ox who is looking for an ox. You're already sitting on it!

"Do you think that I am hiding It from you? There is nothing that I keep from you."—Confucius

There is nothing to master, no need to compete with anything or anyone; there is no need to compare yourself to any standard of measure because, quite simply, whatever you imagine to be lacking or hidden is an illusion. *The drive to improve* is not the type of driving we are interested in here. Instead of going on a wild campaign to change yourself (the "if only" syndrome—if only I could change this or that I would be happy), you simply need to acknowledge and employ what you already have. Zen stipulates that our essential skills are not imprisoned; the problem is that we *believe* that they are. Zen claims there is no first step, no beginning, no "path" to this knowledge or skill or deliverance; there is nothing "to do." This understanding, as Hubert Benoit puts it, "is the great secret, and at the same time the great indication that the Zen Masters reveal to us."

Our Mechanical Inheritance

The bottom line is that driving is an extension of our natural-self. This innate ability is certainly no mystic Zen secret. In our technologically oriented world, people know how to drive before they get behind the wheel for the first time! Even the vice-president of the California Driving School agrees. He told me, "What we are teaching people is to take the *knowledge they already possess* and put it together with that four thousand pounds of iron and steel that they are going to someday control. We want them to know that the steering wheel is an extension of their hands, and that braking will come naturally because the foot is one of the most highly developed sensory areas of the body. In essence, we're refining people's motor skills through the driving of an automobile." We are using and refining skills and talents we grew up with.

"Without raising a foot we are there already. The tongue has not moved, but the teaching is finished."—Mumonkan

We are raised in a world of perpetual motion and mechanical gadgetry, riding in our parents' cars, riding our bikes, skateboards, and go-carts, so that by the time we are old enough to accost our high school driving instructors with our scary presence, our inner gyroscopes are nearly perfectly balanced. By our sixteenth birthday we are all nearly journeymen of the road.

At least I was—or so I thought. Before the time I actually got a driver's license I had logged a good many hours behind the wheel. Whenever my parents went to parties or out to dinner I would gather up my friends and take our other car, a Pontiac Tempest station wagon, out for a spin around the neighborhood and beyond. I was always a little tentative for the first few blocks, but as I look back what I remember is how confident I was on my forbidden adventures. And what freedom!

My favorite place to go, and this impressed my friends the most, was out to a vacant dirt field. There we would spin donuts, kicking up rooster tails of dust. (Afterward we went to the coin-operated car wash, so my parents were getting a cleaner car than they had when they left.)

As I saw it, all this made me a much better driver; after all, you are one alert driver when you are driving along in your Pontiac Tempest station wagon with the thought constantly ticking in the back of your brain of what your Dad is going to do to you if he catches you. But in all honesty, I never figured he'd be too mad, because joyriding in your parents' car is, all said and done, a male rite of passage.

I once told this story to my friend Cathy, adding that this explains why men are usually better drivers than women. She didn't cotton to this notion too well. She said she became a good driver simply by riding and observing in her parents' cars for many years. She said she was just as confident and at ease as I was when she first got her driver's license, and that her confidence grew naturally from her exposure to driving, not from cruising the streets at night like a juvenile delinquent. She said she may not know how to do donuts, but then she didn't see how such a deficiency would hold her back much in life. And I must admit that to this day Cathy is an excellent and safe driver, one of the few people with whom I feel perfectly at ease while sitting in the passenger seat. She helped me shove aside some of my sexist notions, and helped convince me that everyone, men and women alike, are perfectly capable of realizing their innate potential for driving with skill and enjoyment.

"There is nothing lacking in you and you yourself are no different from the Buddha," the Fourth Patriarch, an old-timer named Tao-hsin, tells us. "There is no other way of achieving Buddhahood than letting your mind free to be itself."

One Drives as One Lives

But all this "nothing to do because you already got it" stuff bothered the hell out of Dogen (1200-1253), Japan's first native Zen Master. As a young, impetuous monk he would ask, "Why do we have to practice Buddhism if we already have the Buddha nature?"

Why read this book and practice Zen Driving if we already naturally have the essential driving whammy?!

Dogen traveled to China to seek his answer. We merely have to take a drive on any street or highway and observe ourselves, because in actual driving practice our natural skills, mechanical and otherwise, seem to take a back seat. Feeling angry and crowded in downtown traffic we drop out of accord with our surroundings. Fellow drivers become the enemy, the road turns into an obstacle course, and we end up none too happy with ourselves. In these instances, something prevents us from becoming the Zen Drivers that we actually are. Even though our essential self is in good shape—it could learn to drive the Grand Prix—layers of conditioned images often destroy our innate ability. These are not just bad driving habits, or the failure to develop good driving manners, but aspects of personality (delusions and attachments) that act as layers or filters over the way we drive.

The experts who study driving theorize that "one drives as one lives." They maintain that driving behavior is merely a manifestation of personality. They prove this statistically by showing that the vast majority of accidents are caused by driver error and by equating errant driving behavior and accident rate with individual personality variables. For example, one particular personality that seems to be involved in a large percentage of fatal accidents (especially important since this is the type of personality to abuse alcohol) is the arrogant driver, one who is aggressive, overconfident, forceful, and impulsive. Another study, among college students, portrays the accident-prone personality as being poor in citizenship, with antisocial tendencies, negativistic attitudes, irresponsible behavior, and poor school socialization.

It has been further claimed that driving provides an outlet for basic social and personal expression, allowing us our only opportunity to be in complete control; free to express at will or whimsy our personalities. But if cars are merely moving encasements of our personalities, as zoologist Desmond Morris once maintained, then we are in big trouble.

I don't think any of us need long, dry case studies to prove this. (Which, by the way, doesn't stop scholars from writing them or researchers like me from reading them.) Most of us can tell stories of friends or acquaintances who left their homes in their cars in a bad mood and came back in the front seat of a tow truck or the backseat of an ambulance. I could tell many a tale of Dale, a calm man with a bad temper, who usually resolved conflicts by hitting things: walls, tables, people. And if he was in a bad mood in his car, he was no different. He's wrecked more cars than the Dukes of Hazzard.

Images of the UnZe

Much of personality is a skein of images: images of who we are (self-images), images of who we should be, images of our relationship with the world and others. All carry an emotional charge, and all are the result of past conditioning and thought. We're attached to these images because we mistakenly believe these image-attachments to be our true identity and security.

Image-attachments cloud our natural-self as if polluting a clear pond of water. The object is to keep our pool, our mind, clear and reflective, empty of all pollutants. The historical Buddha felt that all suffering was the direct result of attachment. Aitkin Rioshi says that, "Attachment, as the Buddha used the term, is a blind response to some action in the past." We are a jumble of attachments conditioned by past experiences, ruled by images and thoughts we scarcely realize dictate our actions. All soon become nothing less than blind responses to our environment or circumstances. "Conditioned automatic response patterns," they're called. C.A.R.P., for short, carp, those junk fish that infiltrate our clear, still pond, swimming around, growing bigger, muddying the water, and demanding to be fed! We are influenced by what swims around inside us. We are influenced by our thoughts. Image-attachments affect perception—how we see—and how we see ourselves or a situation determines how we will react. Carlos Castaneda said in a recent interview, "The task with which Don Juan fulfilled me was that of breaking, little by little, my perceptive prejudices."

A monk once asked Master Chao-chou, "How should I use the twenty-four hours of the day?"

Chao-chou replied, "You are used by the twenty-four hours. I use the twenty-four hours."

As the saying goes: You don't think thoughts, thoughts think you.

Image-attachments fragment you from your natural-self. This is the Zen meaning of delusion—the deluded notion that you are separate from others and the world. A sense of wholeness is broken. And without a sense of wholeness and acceptance of your natural-self, you're prone to uncertainty; suddenly, you're afraid, you're in doubt, you're compulsive, you're rageful, you're depressed, you're confused. In driving, to lose contact with your natural free-flowing self can be disastrous. For eventually you get caught in your own idiosyncratic world; not only do you lose self-acceptance and self-confidence, you lose connection with all that is going on around you.

A highway patrolman relates the tale of how, parked at the side of the Ventura Freeway in Los Angeles (the busiest freeway in the United States), he happened to look up to see an older women in a Chrysler LeBaron come barreling down the far left lane. He watched as the woman, ignoring all warning barriers, went flying into the marked-off left lane full of men working! Obviously confused, unable to understand her lane was closed, she continued through the entire construction site, orange plastic cones strewn left and right, the startled CalTrans workmen literally leaping through the air to save their lives. The patrolman jumped into his cruiser and finally caught the woman a mile or two down the freeway. Rolling down her power window but halfway she peered out. "I did something wrong, didn't I?" she said. And when the officer told her, she replied shakily that yes, she saw them—"the poor men!"—but once locked into that particular lane she didn't know how to

get out of it! She was weeping as the patrolman tried to decide what to do with her.

Unlike the woman frozen in panic and conflict, we want to maintain contact with our
free-wheeling natural-selves. We don't want
to be "locked into" anything. Our personality
is a whirlwind of ideas, beliefs, fears, view-
points, response patterns, and complexes
handed to us from the past. And naturally, in
part, these traits go to make up who we are
and how we live. But often personality traits
are like distorting filters, and wouldn't it be a
relief if we could clear them away every once
in a while? Babe Ruth was a colorful personality off the field, but at the moment the
pitcher released the ball you can be assured
Babe Ruth was nothing but experience and
awareness.

And that's how we want to be in traffic. We
need to do away with fragmenting personality
images. As we've seen, these image-attachments can color a traffic situation in adverse
ways, conjuring up excessive emotion, causing gaps in attention. We don't want to find
ourselves wrapped in a brightly colored exo-
skeleton of iron, isolated, whirling through
traffic to the tune of whatever song our personality happens to be playing. This hardly

qualifies as basic expression. And again this is not the song we're listening for.

Pure Appearance

According to Zen, everything is enlightenment from the beginning. Things are as they are. Another word for Buddha is "Tathāgata," which, roughly translated, means "pure appearance." Tathāgata is the essence of living fact—the pure *suchness* of things. Thoughts, image-attachments, automatic response patterns, philosophic mind chatter of any kind interfere with pure appearance. A Zen story translated by Paul Reps tells of one Hogen, a Chinese Zen teacher who lived alone in the country.

One day four traveling monks dropped in on Hogen and asked if they could make a fire in his yard to warm themselves. While they were building the fire, Hogen overheard them arguing about subjectivity and objectivity. He joined them and said, "There is a big stone sitting over there. Do you consider it to be inside or outside your mind?" One of the monks, considered the brightest of the four, stood and said confidently, "From the Buddhist viewpoint everything is an objectification of mind, so I would say that stone is inside my mind." "Hmmm," observed Hogen. "Your head must feel very heavy if you're carrying around a stone like that inside it."

That is, a stone is a stone is a stone.

Maya

Images of personality are what the Zen Buddhists call *maya*, illusion—illusion, in that, compared to one's true nature, they really do not exist. In reality, they are but flimsy ribbons of imagination, never a part of our lives except to the extent that we cling to them and haul them around with us wherever we go.

It is this notion of illusion that points out how we eventually rid ourselves of these cumbersome images—we're rid of them already, since they never existed in the first place! A nifty Zen artifice, but an important one, for though we are aware of the niggling automatic response patterns and image-attachments that plague our driving, we can strive and spend a fortune trying to eradicate them. The Zen method of direct-pointing bypasses this lumbering effort by taking the focus *off* what is *wrong* and putting it *on* what is *right*. What has been right from the beginning.

Awareness and Experience

Personality, good or bad, has nothing to do

with driving. Driving has to do with, quite simply, awareness and experience. In driving there is only an unbroken but discontinuous stream of moments of experience and awareness—unbroken in that no moment, like no snowflake, is like any other.

If you can truly be aware of where you are at this moment and experience everything there is to experience within this moment of space and time called "now," then you are "seeing into your natural-self." And in Zen lingo, to see into our natural-self means to use it—to put it into action.

Natural-self is what remains when you still your mind and ignore all the images of personality. Following this, natural-self relies only on experience and awareness in its interaction with the world. Through experience and awareness you gain access to your natural driving ability, and through further experience and awareness you gain confidence in your natural ability, until, finally, you are that ability.

Experience and awareness may, in fact, be all that natural-self is made up of. No one is quite sure what natural-self happens to be. Like a virtual particle in physics, it cannot be seen, only inferred through experimental interaction. And no big-game-hunting psychologist has ever been successful in bagging a natural-self. No natural-self will fit into a specimen jar.

In Eugene Herrigel's *Zen in the Art of Archery*, the author/apprentice asks the Zen Master, "Who or what is this 'It?' " And the Master replies, "Once you have understood that, you will have no further need of me. And if I tried to give you a clue at the cost of your own experience, I would be the worst of teachers and would deserve to be sacked! So let's stop talking and go on practicing."

TWO

*How
to Use It:
Moving
Meditation*

*"At this moment
what is there you lack!"*

—Hakuin

Direct-Pointing

Zen Driving is effortless and spontaneous, the nondeliberate action of "non-action." Zen Driving is letting "it" do the driving *(Relax and leave the driving to "it.")* But how do we actually tap into it? How do we use our natural-self in order to be Zen Drivers?

"Don't think about it," my father would tell me every time I set out to do a task, "just do it!"

As we unfold our ability as a Zen Driver, it's imperative that we not get bogged down in thoughts, in mere words and instructions. D.T. Suzuki says that "Zen never explains but indicates." By direct-pointing, Zen hopes to sidestep confusion. When the Master shows you the moon by pointing his finger skyward, the object is not to mistake the finger for the moon.

This book is that pointing finger, but it is not pointing toward the moon. It is pointing toward that mechanical device sitting out there next to the curb. Go out there and get in it.

Slip into Something Comfortable

Sit behind the wheel, relax, take a few deep breaths, and realize that all further progress is now in your hands: the vehicle of instruction is the vehicle you're sitting in.

Begin by making a mental note of the fact that you are now in a completely different environment. Become mindful: look around you, acclimate to your surroundings, acknowledge where you are—here, encased in a large cozy machine that for all practical purposes is an extension of yourself. Think of you and your car as one unit. As in fencing, where the foil is an extension of your arm, its tip as sensitive as your fingers, your car becomes a full-body extension of yourself. As you strap on your seat belt you are quite literally *putting on* your car.

Sit there quietly, peacefully plopped in your seat, your hands on the wheel at (as on a clock) ten of two, your feet resting near the pedals. Before entering traffic and making a flurry of decisions, you need to find a center in yourself, an ease, a calm base. You need to get a little here-nowness started in order to slip into the natural rhythm of your natural-self—a discipline, and a practice, known as meditation *(zazen)*, the linchpin of Zen Buddhism.

Ease into the quiet, here-now rhythm of your natural-self and you are slipping into *who you are.* "All meditation," to quote Hugh L'Anson Fausset, "is based in the conviction that we have only to acknowledge and assent to the reality from which we have never in essence been separated."

A Clear Mind, No Thought

In order for your natural-self to shine through, you need a clear mind. To this effect, start your car, and as it warms up, let pass from your mind whatever it was you were previously doing. Arguing with your spouse, beating your dog, sharing a joke with friends—let it pass. Let pass, too, your intended destination. Wherever you're headed, to school, to work, to the dentist—stay put! Whatever comes rolling into your head, simply acknowledge it and then let it pass on by. You want a still mind, clear of all inner chatter. *There is clear awareness in the tranquility of no-thought.*

You also want to be clear of all the shoulds and should-nots of driving. No more techniques that rely heavily on thinking, on memorization and control; methods that despite their seemingly good advice are self-defeating. If you've ever been to traffic school and seen the short film on the Smith method of driving, you'll know what I mean. In that film, the driver, in a nondescript, dirty, white van is demonstrating the five "keys" of the Smith method while driving through a busy town. But he's concentrating so hard on achieving the perfect Smith method that he appears chronically constipated. You immediately get the feeling that you would not want to be a passenger with this fellow.

In Zen Driving, if you can get out of your own way, all the hard work will be done unconsciously. As the psychologist Joseph Chilton Pearce tells us, "God works and man plays—or that is the way the biological scheme is set up and meant to be." When you actually get to driving along, encountering one situation after another, the unconscious process ("God" to some; *dharma* or the "law" to Buddhists) runs something like this: sensation-perception-decision-response. Perception is especially pivotal in this progression, for our unconscious ability to make sensible decisions depends on how we automatically apprehend the raw sensory material flooding our brains; in other words, what *meaning* we place on that raw material. And the meaning or coloring we attach to that input is based on our conditioning—our conjectures, our concepts, our *thoughts*. Aitken Roshi, said, "For subtle realization, it is of the utmost importance that you cut off the mind road."

The task is to efface all distractions, both inner and outer. (Although I have absolutely no proof, I'm inclined to guess that those cars plastered with cute and clever bumper stickers transport drivers whose minds are constantly aswarm with thoughts and opinions—inner bumper stickers.) *No thought, no mind, no form*—that is our task. Jettison all thoughts, images, ideas, opinions, expectations, conceptualizations, and familiarities. Clear your mind and let you be you—that "you" which is perfectly okay, full of vital energy, on schedule, hooked-up, undisturbed, and able to handle whatever comes up no matter what the circumstances.

"What is meditation?" asks the seventh century Zen Master Hui-neng. "It is not to be obstructed in all things. Not to have any thought stirred up by outside conditions of life, good or bad."

Put "It" into Gear

So now, take your clear, quiet mind and put it, and your car, into gear and head off down the street. As you wind your way down one residential street after the other, remember Akihisa Kondo's description of meditation: it's single-minded attention to what you're doing. "It is a sheer act of faith in oneself!" Bolstered by single-mindedness and an unremitting faith in yourself, drive along and do . . . simply . . . nothing.

There will be plenty of discipline and practice to follow (the actual "machinations" of Moving Meditation), but for now just drive as you normally would. What you are doing, bad habits or fears or hesitations notwithstanding, is fine. All driving is pretty much automatic; thought and deliberate action are not necessary. Just drive along. Without instruction, you are practicing or approaching what the Zennists call *wu-wei*, "non-action." In non-action, as Ruth Fuller Sasaki comments, "one does not cease to act, but one's activities arise spontaneously out of the eternal flow of the activity of 'it,' which is not only in accord with, but *is*."

The Grace of It

The fact is, as adult drivers, we already possess a working knowledge of this non-action quality; we are probably just not aware of it. Most of us have plenty of practice behind the wheel, and for the majority of time we are like Zen Masters of fencing *(kendo)* in that the actual mechanics of the task are second nature. We do not become obsessed with just how far we must turn the wheel to maneuver that tight turn, or worry about how much pressure to apply to the brakes to stop for that red light. Likewise the Zen swordsman is not obsessed with maintaining the proper angle of his sword while parrying or advancing. For if he was, he would lose awareness of his opponent's moves—with unfortunate results! (A sort of *kendo* fenderbender.) The experienced swordsperson and driver have achieved a kind of "grace," which is the ability to respond to every situation naturally and confidently.

One of the best descriptions of grace—the essence and elation of doing something without thinking about it—comes from the neurologist and writer, Oliver Sacks. Sacks seriously injured his leg in a hiking accident, though doctors assured him that with the proper physical therapy he would have no trouble walking again. Try as he might, though, Sacks was getting nowhere with the exercises. He became utterly frustrated with his attempts to "will" himself to walk again. Then, one day out of the blue, Sacks was "quickened into life" by an inner music, and took his first few important steps. Later, he wrote:

> The joy of sheer doing—its beauty, its simplicity—was a revelation: it was the easiest, most natural thing in the world—and yet beyond the most complex of calculations and programs. Here, in doing, one achieved certainty with one swoop, by a grace which bypassed the most complex mathematics, or perhaps embedded and transcended them. . . . What was it then, that came suddenly back? It was the triumphal return of the quintessential living "I" . . . not the ghostly, cogitating, solipsisitic "I" of Descartes, which never feels, never acts, *is* not, and *does* nothing; not this, this impotence, this mentalistic fiction. What came, what announced itself, so palpably, so gloriously, was a full-bodied vital feeling and action, originating from an aboriginal, commanding, willing "I." . . . This new, hyper-physical principle was Grace. . . . It made the next move obvious, certain, natural. Grace was the prerequisite and essence of all doing.

It's essential to note that as adult drivers we normally don't think about what we're doing while driving—which, like walking, is exactly how it should be. Researchers tell us, for instance, that the average city driver makes about two hundred decisions a mile. In Los Angeles, drivers log a cumulative eighty-six million miles a day on the freeways alone. Imagine the traffic ruin that would result if every driver worried and thought about his or her every maneuver.

But an even greater danger lies in allowing our natural inner ability to remain unacknowledged. If never fully cultivated, grace has a tendency to slip away, or worse, be forgotten altogether. "What is fatal to one's progress," announces Roshi Kapleau, "is loss of faith in the Buddha's assurance that each of us is inherently pure and whole and is able, through discipline and practice, to realize this innate perfection."

Discipline and Practice: Moving Meditation

In driving, the discipline that is guaranteed to lead us to this graceful perfection is called *Moving Meditation*. This discipline takes a certain amount of hard work, yet if we can muster the motivation to practice it for a

while, say ten or fifteen minutes per outing,
we can be assured of being a happier, safer,
more mindful and efficient driver—a Zen
Driver.

Moving Meditation is essentially a way of
framing what we already have. Grace, after
all, is often a very subtle substance, and we
could use a well-defined discipline to remind
ourselves of its presence—as well as a way of
remaining aware that grace *is not* ego/person-
ality. Moving Meditation is a practice that allows room for our natural-self to unfold, while
filtering out image-attachments and other delusions that would rush in if given half a
chance. It is, so sayeth the Diamond Sutra,
"not dwelling on any object, yet the mind
arises."

This arising mind gives way to our two basic
guides to achieving true Zen Driving: awareness and experience. Moving Meditation, then,
is what helps us get in touch with, improve,
and heighten awareness/experience. Trusting
our natural-self, practicing Moving Meditation, we focus on being *aware* of everything
around us, while we experience, *feel*, everything we do and everything that happens
around us.

No Seeing

With a clear, still mind, free of all "perceptual prejudices," we are nothing but pure awareness/experience. What we're creating with Moving Meditation is a new way of perceiving, practicing what in Zen is called *no seeing*. That is, we look—simply observe—without qualification. "When seeing is no seeing there is real seeing," Suzuki tells us. Real seeing is when we forgo any "specific act of seeing into a definitely circumscribed state of consciousness."

To practice Moving Meditation you must fully accept where you now find yourself, here in your car. Divest yourself of all expectation, standards of comparison and technique, take that clear, observing, unobstructed state of being, and keep on driving! Now, instead of sitting erect and attentive in a quiet stationary place like a Zendo or meditation hall, you are now sitting erect and attentive in your moving vehicle. You are now meditating as you move along. Do not be ruled by anything inside or outside of you. See and experience without intrusion, but when an intrusion does rear its ugly head in the form of anger, an opinion, some driver cutting you off, simply acknowledge the stray image and return your focus to being aware of everything around you. Now, driving along, be intimately involved in the action and be aware that everything around you is happening for the first time. Everything is constantly changing, each traffic situation requiring its own set of responses. Nothing is left to rote. Keep your mind, body, and senses wide awake, and as you drive along know that all that you *see* is as new as a baby's smile, no matter how many times you *think* you have seen it before.

Real or TV?

Using this newfangled vision allows you to realize that everything beyond your windshield has never happened before, does not fit into any concept, any thought, any memory image; each moment is one of ongoing, first-hand discovery. Practicing Moving Meditation allows you to experience your here-now involvement in all of the action around you. It's only when you lose your immediate awareness and experience that a black veil hangs over your perceptions, causing you to revert back to old patterns and images, transforming your windshield into a TV screen. As with TV, you are then sitting separate from what you are watching. And like everything on TV, what you see from behind the wheel appears either preprogrammed (a product of the past) or rehearsed and minutely structured. Conversely, by practicing Moving Meditation while driving, everything is seen as happening now, fresh, for the first time. But to the extent that your perceptions of what lies beyond your windshield are preprogrammed by thought—laden by conditioned image-filters—you are then that much removed from the actual driving experience. What you are then seeing, and acting upon, might as well be a TV program.

As you drive through your immediate neighborhood everything seems familiar: you stare out of your car and feel that you have seen this particular show a thousand times before. Same old homes, same streets, same kids, same sky, same earth, same problems, same grind. Every view is imbued with endless memories and associations, things that originate solely inside your head and color your perceptions. These images dilute your awareness, take you out of the immediate experience of your surroundings, and make your trip, short as it may be, unsatisfying and boring: a rerun. Also, considering that most accidents occur on "familiar" terrain, driving passively through your neighborhood can be a bit on the dangerous side.

A Bubble of Perception

Driving in your car, traveling through a TV show of your own making, is similar to what Castaneda's Don Juan referred to as operating from a "bubble of perception." According to the old sorcerer, we live inside a sphere or bubble, its inside surface as smooth and polished as a mirror, ". . . and what we witness on its round walls is our own reflection. . . . The thing reflected is our view of the world. That view is first a description, which is given to us from the moment of our birth until all our attention is caught by it and the description becomes a view."

For many drivers, getting in their cars is not an opening of awareness and experience, but is like climbing into a bubble of perception.

For many weeks I worked with a middle-aged woman named Lorrie, trying to help her dissolve her bubble of perception. She was an easily excitable, dramatic person with a critical, sometimes biting nature. Driving around town with Lorrie seemed uneventful; that is, until she went over forty-five miles per hour, when, for all intents and purposes, she drove straight into another world. (I learned that Lorrie usually went out of her way to avoid all freeways, and drove other drivers crazy by never going over forty-five on the open road.)

When I asked Lorrie to describe what it was like to go over forty-five, she replied that "everything was filled with a bunch of blurry shapes. I don't know, they're going real fast, and sometimes they seem to dart right in front of me. Everything's hazy. It's scary. Know what I mean?" No, I had to admit, I didn't. I couldn't assume to know what things looked and felt like from inside her head. I said I had never driven in such a place. "It's not some foreign land," she retorted.

But, indeed, it was. This foreign land, where she infrequently visited, had specific, palpable effects on Lorrie. Her chest felt constricted and she became short of breath. Her hands would tingle and her whole body felt very hot and flushed. She became convinced that she would soon end up either having a heart attack or getting in a wreck. Like many people who suffer from phobias, Lorrie's fear of going over forty-five was metaphoric of something unconscious in her personality. I was no medicine man, I told her, but I did believe that by practicing Moving Meditation I would not only help her become a safer, more efficient driver (which is why she came to me in the first place), but also take some of the sting out of her phobia.

I will return to Lorrie in a little bit. I have

introduced her here as a reminder that the best way to break out from under the influence of strong image-attachments, like phobias, is through Moving Meditation. That is, when overcome or overrun by these images and feelings the object is to realign yourself with awareness/experience: focus on being aware of all that is around you, experience everything without qualification. In reality, this is who you are, and from this you operate. Now, though, I want to explore in finer detail awareness and experience, our all-important two-pronged approach to Moving Meditation and Zen Driving. Ultimately, you will realize that awareness and experience are both part of one reciprocal process (you're aware of what you're experiencing; you experience— feel—what fills your awareness), but for the purposes of exploration and explanation, let's tease them apart.

A Samurai Awareness

Beginning with awareness, the discipline and practice is simply to *focus* on maintaining a 360-degree picture of everything around you at all times. Be aware that you are driving in a multidimensional reality where things are happening on every conceivable level. Sustain a full samurai 360-degree watch. Be aware of any and all possible situations. Let precious little escape your attention. Be aware of your speed, your surroundings; stretch your awareness in all directions, as far ahead, as far behind, and as far to the sides as you can see. There is no trick to developing this degree of awareness, nothing fancy in its use. You quite simply do whatever you need to do to sustain it. Keep glancing in the rearview and side mirrors, turn your head, turn your whole body; do, in fact, whatever's comfortable, just as long as you retain that 360-degree picture in your head. Just as long as you know as certainly as you can know anything exactly what is ahead of you and around you at any given instant!

This awareness is always a here-now affair. Awareness goes from instant to instant; you never anticipate or assume you know what another driver is going to do, for that is slipping out of awareness and into troublesome thought, which is how you get bushwacked! You cannot think your way out of a situation; thought is a thousand times *slower* than natural-self, non-action a thousand times *quicker* than deliberate action. Nothing can match the alacrity, acumen, decisiveness, and alertness of natural-self. And all you need to do to have it is to use it!

Be aware—focus on awareness.

Take account of and gather into your pure awareness everything outside you, everything within your field of vision and senses, anything that in the slightest way comes within the proximity of the skin of your car. Be aware of the sights and sounds and feelings in your path and slipstream. The white lines and Botts Dots that make your tires bump when you cross them. The shapes and shades of the cars keeping pace with you. Be aware of the color of traffic lights as far ahead as your vision carries. What is the traffic scene ahead of you? Behind you? Who's walking the sidewalks? In what direction do the shadows of the trees fall? How briskly is the wind blowing? How close are you to other cars? All this happens spontaneously as you drive along and practice Moving Meditation: you don't latch onto any of it. Nothing sticks in your mind, but nothing escapes it. Watch the eyes of the other drivers. Keep up a "running commentary" on the activity around you: the Mustang twenty feet behind you, gaining; the blue Toyota forty feet behind you, dropping back; the truck one hundred feet ahead of you, changing lanes; the motorcycle you hear on your tail to the left; that kid on the bike approaching an upcoming intersection; the dog in the window of that white house, just sitting there, watching.

No one can teach you this awareness. All you need is the intention or motivation and you will automatically do it. The mind is fully capable of retaining a circular picture while in motion; you don't have to physically look in any one particular direction at any one particular instant to know what's there. Just keep up a constant vigilance and your mind will "remember" a full moving picture. This ability allows you to move comfortably and fluidly through traffic, and, just in case, provides an out for quick emergencies. Accidents are, in theory, out there waiting for you. According to the Traffic Safety Council, two of the top four causes of automobile accidents are inattention and improper lookout—in different terms, poor awareness. If, however, you actively maintain the level of awareness implied by Moving Meditation, you automatically *know* what is out there waiting. You know where it is, you know how far away it is, and since all is in motion, you are able automatically to calculate how long it takes before all things converge.

But you not only want to be aware of what's going on outside of you, you also want to tune in to what is taking place inside of you. Be aware as you drive along of what comes up as extraneous mind chatter, especially those opinions, judgments, criticisms, and emotional valences stirred up by the action around you. Here are a few of the more common ones: "What a jerk!" "You bimbo!" "The light doesn't get any greener, buddy!" "Go any slower, lady, and you might as well walk!" All this incessant inner prattle moves you off center and out of your natural-self. Be aware of self-judgments as well. Go easy on yourself. Keep your focus on your surroundings.

Be aware, additionally, of all associations. For example, as you drive by this pretty little city park here on your right, it may remind you of an old sweetheart. Later, when Zen Driving is second nature to you, you will enjoy your memory; but, for now, the object is to establish and augment natural-self by acknowledging the memory or association and letting it go.

Experience

Naturally, this high degree of awareness does not depend upon some rarefied gymnastics of the mind—everything that's happening around you must also be *felt*. So not only must you be aware of all that is going on, but you must at the same time *experience* all that is happening. By this I mean the full mind-body sensation of every facet of driving, both outer and inner. Driving is as much a physical sensation as it is a mental one.

Be so attuned to the cars around you that you can actually feel them. Feel them closing in, falling back, boxing you in. Feel yourself accelerate away from them. Know how the highway feels, the uneven macadam, the ruts, the smooth pavement, the wet rainy roads, the hum of the steel bridge.

What feelings do the city's architecture stir? What smells waft by? What do you hear? The engine? The wind? The drone of traffic? The blare of a teenager's radio? Experience how your car genuinely feels in your hand: the vibrations and tingle of the steering wheel; the friction of the tires on the road's surface; the weight and maneuverability of the car. How quick is it? How sluggish? Feel that turn coming up. Feel yourself lean into it. Feel your speed. Sense your foot on the accelerator or brake; feel the car's motion. Feel your body tighten in the seat belt as you come to a sudden stop; feel the force of gravity as you leap away from a stop light.

It is this experiential sense, this *being fully there*, nearly impossible to describe, that makes driving something special, something you can slip into as comfortably as though the road was custom-made for you.

Continue driving, and meanwhile check in on what's happening in the inner world. Are you late for an appointment? Do you feel anxious? Is traffic so jammed that you feel frustrated? What does the rush of adrenaline feel like when that fellow runs a stop sign just ahead of you? What about anger—are you going to hang on to it? All these feelings, especially anger and fear, have the potential, if indulged, of getting you "out of 'it.' " They take you out of your natural-self (pure awareness/experience). They poke large holes in your Moving Meditation and make driving a chore and not a joy; the road, no longer custom-made, becomes an aggravating obstacle course. So when these intruders pop up, you must snap back. Return to the discipline of Moving Meditation—be aware of, experience, and acknowledge the intruders, then let them go, once again returning your focus to the sights and sensations of driving.

The Discipline of Practice

With a degree of faith and trust in the practice of Moving Meditation we reach that level of "full presence participation" where we become our surroundings and are then driving from a new order of things. It is from this new order of participation that our abilities as a Zen Driver are so much second nature to us that we can drive out of difficult situations as easily as scratching an itch.

All this is simple and straightforward, but at times, it's easier said than done. It's practice that takes hard work. And for some, such as Lorrie, Moving Meditation becomes quite an ordeal.

I started with Lorrie by pointing out how her perceptions were influenced by thoughts and conditionings. But instead of insinuating or saying that something was wrong with her (you're a lousy driver, you're phobic) I asked her to get in touch with what was right. I asked her to make the effort to practice Moving Meditation as she drove around town: to focus on staying aware and experiencing without qualification her driving environment and herself. I said that when things became scary she needed to accept this frightening world, to explore it. "You're learning to trust yourself," I said. "And that *you* that you are trusting is more than you imagine—with experience and awareness it will expand! In other words, you'll improve naturally over the course of constant practice." I wanted her not to run from her fears, but to be aware of them and experience them. In this way she would challenge her inhibitions and build up a tolerance to feelings that she *assumed* she could not bear and so had to avoid.

After she was familiar with driving from a quiet, meditative place in herself, we experimented with short jaunts on the freeway. I picked times when the freeway was relatively empty, and taped a card over the speedometer so that she experienced driving, its speed and feel, on its own terms, free of all external monitors. I wanted her to drive relying solely on experience and awareness, and go face-to-face with her inner monitors and images of fear, vulnerability, and senses of success and failure.

Lorrie, at first, naturally kept her speed low. But eventually, in small increments, she increased her speed, felt the rush of emotion and the beginnings of a panic attack; then, when she'd endured all she could endure, she backed off by slowing down. This went on for session after session. Finally the fear transformed itself into other feelings: at times sadness, at others something akin to amazement and elation, all equally scary at first, but soon acknowledged. At the end of our work together, Lorrie was able to drive the freeways at any population density, and she was able to tolerate, then let pass, whatever feelings arose, keeping her focus on awareness/experience.

Acceptance and Assertion

If we can stay in pure awareness/experience, maintaining our Moving Meditation practice, then eventually we will lay the foundation for two very important aspects of driving: acceptance and assertion. As an outgrowth of focusing on awareness and experience, we as drivers can learn to tap into and *accept* that we are all interconnected and form one body as we travel through traffic; and, simultaneously, realize and *assert* our individual ability to maneuver any situation. Again, both of these qualities (the *yin* and *yang* of driving) are brought out by practicing Moving Meditation.

But let's shelve our Moving Meditation for a short time, and pull over and park at the side of the road while we examine these two qualities a little more closely.

The best introduction to the qualities of acceptance and assertion in driving comes from Sean, a longtime San Francisco cabbie. As we talked one night for hours about driving, it became quite clear to me that, though he had never heard the term before, Sean was a genuine Zen Driver.

"It's really important for me to try and be alert out there," he began. "It's like willing myself to be wired. If you drive a cab, it's your business: you're trying to make money.

"People all the time cannot make good decisions. They're confused, and that's because they're trying to think their way out of a situation instead of just reacting. . . . There's always something happening around you in the city. Somebody's going to double park, somebody's going to see a parking spot and back up against traffic. I can see that kind of thing coming and so try not be a chump and get stuck behind it. I can avoid it early by being aware. The long and short of it is, if you drive well you make more money.

"And driving well means I'm driving assuredly. But it's really easy for that assuredness to become aggression. A lot of the old drivers are burned out and they're just too aggressive and uptight. It becomes a little like car warfare out there. If somebody cuts you off, then in the next half-hour or so you're going to be more reactive, more hair-triggered if somebody else pulls something. In a cab it's going to happen to you ten or twenty times a night. Then, some nights, you got to figure it's the moon, something in the air. There're nights when everybody's honking at each other, flipping one another off. There's a lot of hostility out there.

"Driving ideally you shouldn't be worrying about what you're doing at all. You have to do everything second-nature. It's a social contract we're all part of. I have to constantly remember that these people, these drivers, are not *doing it* to me. Maybe they're stupid. Maybe they're unaware. Maybe they're just timid or indecisive. I can't get uptight about that. I can't think they're my enemies.

"Driving really is at its worst when I lose that collective experience of being on the road. I remember driving down California Street once, really angry at things. I was in a bad mood. And this woman behind me was honking her horn. I pulled over in the right lane and she pulled over behind me and was still honking. It was making me *very* angry— so I flipped her off. But she kept honking and pointing. Well, it turned out that my hazard lights were on. She was trying to tell me that. But I assumed she was riding me because I wasn't going fast enough. If I would have just looked at her I would have known that she was trying to do me a favor. I felt terrible.

"When you're out there every day you have

to consider yourself in a stream. And there're only so many things you can do. You may be able to avoid certain floating tree limbs, but you can't move the rocks. Driving then becomes a kind of microcosm for survival. How are you going to approach a certain situation? Aggressively? Negatively? Or are you going to try and enjoy it? Are you going to try and be in a frame of mind where what you're seeing is unavoidable and there is no need to worry about it? That's what I like to do, and try to do, anyway, when I'm driving.''

Sean and I agreed that we need to *accept* the mundane tribulations and situations of driving before we can learn to enjoy them. We need to remain part of the ''one flow,'' the ''collective experience'' of driving. There are a lot of different personalities out there, a lot of different cars traveling at different speeds, exhibiting varying levels of expertise (or lack thereof). We cannot control the highway system. We cannot create our own physical reality. If someone cuts us off, goes slow, makes us angry, we simply must accept it, acknowledge it—then let it pass. In this way we help maintain the highway's harmony.

Now, as you sit there quietly (wherever it is you've parked) and peer through your windshield, realize that acceptance is that quality that helps dissolve the "bubble of perception," that bypasses the mad influx of image-attachments that freeze us in a TV show world.

Oneness

In reality, there is nothing separate, solid, or fixed out there beyond our windshields. According to Zen Buddhism all is one inter-connected flow, constantly changing. You and the world outside your windshield are the same thing. From this, Buddhism holds that there is no actual separate self. It's all just one big process. There is no self, no form, no mind, no thing *(nothing)*, just the great seamless void, *Sunyata.*

To Western ears the above may sound a bit bleak. (What do you mean *no self? No me?*) To understand what I mean without venturing into a great deal of ponderous metaphysics, it's necessary to take a slight excursion into the Zen of Western sciences.

Our excursion leads us initially to the work of Nobel laureate, Ilya Prigogine, whose pio-neering studies in the field of thermodynamics have, not coincidentally, been applied to transportation science, both by himself and the U.S. Department of Transportation, which uses his holistic brand of mathematics to predict traffic flow patterns.

 Prigogine has worked out formulas for a universe where everything, including us humans, is bound by constantly moving, changing, flowing energies. Prigogine believes that the forms of the universe maintain their shapes not as the result of energies that have melted into states of static equilibrium, but because of their symbiotic relationship with the fluctuating environment. Prigogine calls these interconnected forms "dissipative structures," and maintains that they exist and survive only by remaining open to a flowing matter and energy exchange, an interpenetration with the ecology that exists on multitudinous levels—what the mystic Walter Russel called "a rhythmic balanced interchange." A good example would be the existence of a vortex in a river, for the vortex derives its autonomy only from its interchange with the river. According to Prigogine, the greater a structure's autonomy, the more interchange and interdependence there is with the environment. In other words, nothing can exist without its environment.

It's important to accept Priogogine's model of self-organizing structures in constant, dynamic interchange with their surrounding and let go of the illusory idea or image of "things" separate in the world. *(No thing.)* Autonomous forms do not exist separately; their independence is *literally* based on *inter*dependence. Carl Jung put it succinctly when he said that the word *individual* means indivisible, undivided.

A Web of Jewels

In the psychology of Jung, to achieve full individuation means to achieve Self, always with a capital "S," another name for natural-self. "An extreme paradox is contained in Jung's symbol of the Self," Marie-Louis von Franz explains. "It is at once that which is the most intimate, the most individual, and at the same time a mirror of total reality."

Buddhists like to picture what is called the "Net of Indra" when conjuring up notions similar to Jung's. The oneness and interrelatedness of all things is represented by a great *web* extending through all time and universes. At the intersection of each crossing line is a jewel, and within the surface of just one of these crystals lies the reflection of every other crystal in the vast network. Each single jewel reflects every other one, like millions of mirrors facing one another. These endless reflections are independent of one another, yet at the same time they're bound together as one whole.

Fragmentation Creates Conflict

Buddhism agrees implicitly with Prigogine's physics and Jung's psychology in that any consideration of self-sufficiency must be seen in the context of the One. Fragmentation is a delusion, but one all too often assumed to be a fact. Buddhism considers the "self" to be such an assumed fact. "The emphasis on giving importance to the self," insists J. Krishnamurti, "is creating great damage in the world, because it is separative and therefore it is constantly in conflict, not only within itself but with society." Yasutani Roshi says, "The fundamental delusion of humanity is to suppose I am here and you are out there. . . . The practice of Zen is forgetting the self in the act of uniting with something."

You can accept it as fact that a driver is not separate from his or her highway environment. It is an error to *imagine* (to be under the influence of *images*) that when you get in your car you are somehow magically sequestered from your ecology. This sort of divisive thinking causes drivers to exhibit all manner of unruly behavior. Driving is not a conflictual situation; unlike Japanese fencing, there are no opponents. Nevertheless, when the delusion of egotism sets in, separation and anger crop up and suddenly all those other drivers out there *are* opponents.

The Prime Minister Kuo Tze of the Tang Dynasty loved to visit his favorite Zen Master. The two got along famously; the Prime Minister displayed no loftiness or vanity, the Zen Master indulged in no exaggerated politeness or deference. One day, however, Kuo Tze asked, "Roshi, how does Zen Buddhism explain egotism?" The Master suddenly glowered, and in a haughty, contemptuous voice said to the Prime Minister, "What are you saying, you numbskull?!" This unexpected defiance outraged Kuo Tze and anger rapidly spread across his face. The Zen Master then looked at the Prime Minister, smiled, and said, "Your Excellency, this is egotism!"

Anger and overly aggressive behavior are the earmarks of separation, an inability to fully accept our undivided nature.

On the highway, a good example of Oneness is when the far left lane ends and traffic must merge. This works wonderfully when, before the lane actually ends, drivers adjust their speeds and merge like two decks of cards shuffled together. In order for this to happen, though, drivers must function in a single un-broken flow. But too often the situation is quite different. Stuck in their Lone Ranger modes, drivers jump lanes ahead of time and jockey for their *rightful territory* and, usually angry, won't let other cars merge in front of them. At those times when individual drivers forget their interconnectedness, each of them acting on individual whims, the flow is re-peatedly broken and traffic snarls to an aggra-vating stop.

In reality, there is no rigid distinction be-tween what our thoughts commonly define as *me* and *all else*. In reality, once we "put on" our car we are entering a larger web of con-nections, the whole movement of the road-car-driver ecosystem. Here we not only become closer to people, we are actually involved in one joint effort, as in one large choreographed dance. The natural rhythm of this dance, this flowing movement of cars and people, is fa-cilitated by the discipline of Moving Medita-tion.

Compassion

Following Moving Meditation, operating from Oneness, we begin to recognize our-selves in other drivers. We begin to feel com-passion *(karuna)*, the stuff of acceptance.

Compassion is the glue that keeps the whole works together. There exists no full expression of our talents as Zen Drivers without compassion. Compassion begins with an unconditional friendliness toward oneself (accepting ourself: tapping into natural-self) and extends to other motorists. And the wonderful thing about compassion is that it is always there. It is only lacking when hardened mental boundaries creep up between us and our environment. It is this artificial separation, this loss of acceptance and compassion, that causes us to judge every other driver on the road, that causes fenderbenders or worse. In Zen Driving, there are no impediments save our own disruptive thoughts; all that anger and frustration, all those bad drivers "out there"—simply acknowledge them as rocks in the stream to be calmly paddled around. As good Zen Drivers, *nothing* can get our goat!

Assertion

Now, having maintained a high level of awareness/experience though the practice of Moving Meditation, we come to accept natural-self and everything that natural-self includes (which is everything). So now, having accepted it, we can assert it!

A caution, however, is in order. A Zen

Driver, is by his or her very own nature, assertive, but you cannot assert Zen Driving (or *any* driving skill for that matter). If you have the gumption to practice Moving Meditation then automatically you'll be more assertive. Assertion is pure intentionality devoid of mental constructs and mental commands. "An assertion is Zen," says Suzuki, "only when it is itself an act and does not refer to anything that is asserted in it." In other words, assertion is not willing ego or a certain talent or ability into action. There is no *I will* in assertion. Assertion just *happens*. When someone swings blindly into your lane, you automatically swing out of the way. You don't say, "Now look at that numbskull pulling in front of me, I think I better switch lanes. Here I go!" By that time the metal is bent and still bending. No Zen Master would ever tell himself or anyone else to be assertive, for that would merely be offering another mental construct. You cannot pull out of your driveway and say, "Now I'm gonna be a Zen Driver! I plan on driving absolutely impeccably this trip!" Because as soon as you start your Moving Meditation, that willing "I" is going to dissolve into the wonderfully efficient *no self* of *non-action*. When we get down to it, Moving Meditation is the shoehorn that fits us into Zen

Driving, which "cannot be taught, it must be caught."

Now, given the above, know that you must be assertive if you're going to be a Zen Driver! Assertion is the resultant force of awareness/experience that kicks our skills into gear! It's the action-energy that makes our abilities unfold *and* improve! Assertion is confidence! It's realizing our capabilities as inherent Zen Drivers! It is showing our ability to respond to every situation! It's the quality of piloting our own ship!

What Makes It Work

Assertion is also what allows traffic, the road-car-driver ecosystem, to operate. For instance, coming upon a stalled car in the middle of a two-lane intersection, what, according to transportation experts, are you supposed to do? Nine out of ten drivers say they would stop behind the stalled car. But in order to avoid entangling the traffic any further it's better to assert yourself (without thinking about it!) and drive around the stalled car.

A Zen Driving riddle: How long will drivers sit at a red light that is broken?

The trouble is: we don't trust often enough in our natural-self, or worse, don't believe it exists at all. Therefore it never gets enacted, much less asserted. But there are times, especially in potentially dangerous situations, when we must automatically assert ourselves. That spontaneous *urge to act* must be there when we need it! To trust in natural-self is to assert it. Through Moving Meditation we will eventually learn to channel our powers of assertion evenly through all of our day-to-day driving situations.

Natural-Self vs. External Control

Assertion is a natural form of awareness. Unfortunately, awareness is more often maintained by worrying whether or not a cop is in the vicinity. Rather than relying on the awareness and assertion of natural-self to dictate our actions, we often look elsewhere.

It's an illusion that the harmony of our roads is maintained by external forces or factors such as road signs, lights, lines, and laws. We come to rely on these external controls, and when something out of the ordinary comes upon us—a broken light, an erratic driver—we frequently become disoriented. Professional driving studies differentiate between what they call drivers who have an "external locus of control" and those with an "internal locus of control." The studies conclude that the latter, who act more independently, are quicker to pick out distinct items embedded in their immediate environment (in other words, their perceptions are sharper) and statistically are better and safer drivers.

The truth is, harmony always begins with the individual, the integrated, "undivided" individual who, with Fritz Perls, knows that "the only control is the situation." This, really, is the only law. It is the thinking behind the best in road engineering. Again it's a popular misconception that things such as traffic lights are safety devices positioned to issue hardened orders to drivers. Actually road engineers regard these devices chiefly as instruments in the production of orderly movement. (It's a favorite joke in New York City that traffic laws are only "guidelines." But that's actually the truth! Everywhere.) Streets and roads are designed to aid the flow of traffic, with safety as a hoped-for byproduct. The final responsibility *always* rests with the individual.

William Garrison, head of the Department of Transportation at U.C. Berkeley, nicely stresses this point. "Suppose everybody drove according to the law," he told me, "that they came to full stops at every stop sign, that they followed one another at two second intervals—traffic wouldn't work. There would be congestion everywhere. . . . Though the roads are a rule-bound system, there is a collective understanding of how things really work."

Professor Garrison adds that the "collective understanding" among individual drivers results from a "remarkable piece of social learning, where individuals and society as a whole have learned to operate their vehicles safely." How that is achieved, he could not refrain from adding, "is beyond me."

It is, perhaps, somewhat surprising to hear a hardcore academic confess to an inexplicable force as the foundation of highway harmony. Yet like many other transportation and driving experts, Professor Garrison sounds a little like a Zen teacher, proffering that external rules and systems are to be assimilated and then subsumed by self-reliance—by natural-self. Zen Master Hui-neng wrote, "When, outwardly, a man is attached to form, his inner mind is disturbed. . . . Those who recognize an objective world, and yet find their mind undisturbed are in true Dhyana (Meditation)."

No Mind, No Form

We know we're in true meditation when there exist *no* mind and *no* form. As you start your car and point yourself back into the One, you *see* from a *clear* place of non-action, where there exist no anxiety, no self-concepts, no perceptual prejudices, no frozen patterns, no image-filters of any kind. There is no mind. From this unclouded, meditative place everything you encounter becomes new, constantly created afresh each moment. And as these experiential moments continue along temporal lines, your ability broadens and expands to the point where the disciplinary form of Moving Meditation is no longer needed. There is no form. Acceptance and assertion and awareness and experience all feed back and fade into one another. Self-consciousness falls like fledgling feathers, and you are meditating whether you know it or not.

Suddenly you're back where you already are: right here, in your car, part of the ecology, paying attention, being centered; driving your car, not riding your thoughts.

As you continue driving through your neighborhood you pass through familiar or curious surroundings that stir up impressions, memories, and associations. You are aware of all these images and thoughts and feelings; you acknowledge them without criticism or judgment, then quickly let them pass. You return your attention to your driving. There is no thought, no mind, no form. "There is neither the self that is sitting, nor the earth which is supporting it.''—Shibayama

You slip through your neighborhood in a state of *samadhi*. You find your favorite on-ramp, slide onto the main thoroughfare, and tuck yourself into the flow of rush hour traffic.

You move in and out of lanes until you feel comfortably situated, then nestle into the vast coursing freeway snake that, as one body, slithers through the city. You watch for the appropriate offramp. You watch the cars ahead of you, aware of everything around you. You are an integral part of the traffic flow, ready to move individually in any direction if need be. You feel just fine; you feel every motion of your car, fully experiencing yourself sitting regally behind the wheel, foot on the pedal, your speed commensurate with the world of cars around you. No images or thoughts or opinions intrude upon your mind. You are one with everything. One with yourself. One with the freeway snake. One with the truck you're following. One with the woman in the Buick on your right . . . The same women who suddenly cuts you off!

And you are one with the adrenaline and anger beginning to speed through your system. You are one with the building reaction to pounce on your horn and give her a piercing blast! But you catch yourself. You let the anger pass without riding it, and ease back into your surroundings. You drive until the traffic finally begins to thin. You leave the freeway and follow an unfamiliar road that eventually narrows and begins to wind through the outskirts of your town.

You switch on the radio. And as the country begins to open around you, green fields and fat full trees, you begin to settle into the music of the ol' Zen Highway: "At this moment what is there you lack!"

THREE

The
Beginning
Driver

"Any knowledge or learning is just like a drop of water fallen in a valley when it is compared with the depth of experience."

—*Tokusan Sengan*

You, the Coach

The neophyte driver sits behind the wheel for the first time. An adolescent or older, he or she is about to gain access to the great American freedom to travel where you will. Eager, frightened, wide-eyed, they look for guidance. Show me how to control this machine, they plead, how to beat this thing into submission.

If you were the Zen Driving coach, what would you tell them? Setting aside the mechanical skills for a moment, I hope you would tell them, based on the guides set forth in the preceding chapter, *nothing*, that is, tell them there are no expectations, there will be no standards of comparison. Your beginning driver may look at you a little askance when you tell him or her that the main point is simply to enjoy (without hitting anything) the driving experience.

Then again, you yourself may be looking at

this book a little askance, wondering how you got to be the driving coach all of a sudden. How can you teach someone something you have just been exposed to yourself? The answer is, you can't. And, for that matter, neither can I "teach" you anything. As I've said before, I can only provide guides and allow you the space to learn for yourself. In Zen, there are no borders between "teacher" and "student"; we are all working together to learn for ourselves.

This is the point I want to stress continually throughout this chapter: I'm hoping that my experiences with beginning and "problem" drivers will be valuable to you as both teacher and student of Zen Driving. It's not with a little modesty that I would like to see Zen Driving spread and take hold throughout our society, and for that reason, would like to see the seeds of Zen Driving planted in adolescence, where they are guaranteed to take root. In the words of Ron McNees, vice-president of the California Driving School, "Teenagers are at the prime of their personal abilities and their reflexes are sharp. Their minds are attuned to driving because it is the cutting of the umbilical cord for them." Further, I have found that teenagers, who are still forging their own identities, who haven't built up image-attachments and fixed concepts, are the ones best capable of driving from their natural-self. We can learn a lot about Zen Driving from the first efforts of teenagers, not the least of which is that the experience of driving is, for them, forever fun.

And yet, as I worked with teenagers and read driver's manuals and statistics about them, I was disheartened to find that, by and large, they are treated with scorn by society and legislative bodies, viewed as a threat on the road, as dangerous outlaws who should be constantly watched and monitored. I was also discouraged to discover, knowing how much teenagers love to drive and love the freedom that driving promises, that driver's training is granted so little importance in the high schools. My spirits lifted, though, after I met Robert Terry, a tireless California lobbyist, who is working to upgrade driver's training in high schools with his excellent competency-based program. A little later I want to tell you about Terry, because I think his program is analogous to Zen Driving, and that, in true Zen fashion, we can benefit from one another.

But for now, let's get you, the driving coach, back in the front seat with your beginner and out in a large, abandoned parking lot. The first thing you want to do, of course, is get your initiate (young or old) to feel comfortable. Tell him/her to rest his/her hands on the steering wheel, (at ''ten of two,'' as on a clock), press the accelerator and brake pedals, click the turn signals, look in the mirrors. You want to give your beginner the sense of being part of the car; you also want to instill confidence and composure. Say there is nothing you can do that is incorrect; nor is there any way you can get hurt. Emphasize the *feel* of the car, nothing else. Show how to start the car, how to put it in gear; sit back, and say, ''Simply drive.''

In the annals of driver's training there is some precedent for what you are doing. One important study by a couple of researchers shows that learning-to-drive teens who spend a majority of their initial time behind the wheel on an open driving range have fewer accidents. Highway patrolmen, stunt and race drivers also train on open ranges. The idea is to gain awareness and experience of various maneuvers without worrying that mistakes will cost you. Training on the open range allows drivers to gain confidence without undue pressure. Worries and anxieties aside, your beginner is able to get a sense of his/her natural ability, which he/she can now take to the streets.

Judy

Judy is a thirty-year-old physical therapist who had her last driving experience on the streets fourteen years ago while still in high school. It's early morning and she and I are sitting in my car in the middle of a vacant shopping mall parking lot. The engine's idling and Judy is telling me of her failure back in her first driver ed class, adding that she has had a phobia of driving ever since. I listen patiently, then tell her it is time to play. "Let's just have fun," I say. "Pay attention to what things feel like. Enjoy yourself—and we'll stop whenever you say the word." And so we begin, fears and all, to explore the huge parking lot.

Judy inches forward, then stops, repeating this bold maneuver several times. Then she begins to circle the parking area, experimenting with turning and stopping and going faster. Reticently, I offer the occasional "good" and "do what you want." After a while, it is apparent she is beginning to have a good time.

Eventually I ask her if she would like to try something a little more fun, a little more adventurous. At moderate speeds I have her suddenly slam on the brakes—just to get the feel of it, and to know what she has at her disposal. Then at a similar speed, shy of skidding, I have her abruptly crank the wheel hard to the right. She practices this same maneuver to the left. She is starting to get the feel of the car, both within and slightly beyond her limits. And with this new awareness, for the last fifteen minutes of our one-hour lesson, I have Judy follow some of the marked lanes in the lot. Earlier I had set up plastic cones, and now ask Judy to go around them, getting as close as possible, even if she has to hit a few of them, which she does.

At her second outing, Judy displays only enthusiasm. Following her third session, we tackle some neighborhood streets, and though she is somewhat tentative and overly cautious (which is fine!), Judy says she is no longer afraid of driving. In fact, she tells me she honestly enjoys driving. By our fourth session, she is chattering away about buying a new car.

But what kind of car does Judy want to buy?

Many of the recent car commercials on television are eager to stress and wild to sell you the high performance abilities of their new machines. (No problem for Judy, who these days now finds car commercials the most exciting and appealing thing on TV.) Car commercials, through their ad agencies, are really selling unbounded enthusiasm—enthusiasm for driving, enthusiasm for life. Skirring along a curving mountain road, dancing around obstacles, overtaking and sailing past sluggish competitors. Speed, agility, command of the highway, these are the new good looks of the new automobiles. What BMW, for example, is really marketing is confidence and an alive feel of the car and the road. And if all this sounds a bit Zen, it is! It is getting in touch with the full expression of your driving prowess.

Warning! Humans Ahead

And yet it is this very expression that worries many driving professionals and legislators, who are concerned, as one professional driving instructor put it, "that the more a person learns and knows about controlling the car, the harder it is for them to temper their attitudes toward full expression." And so they are more likely to cause accidents. Human beings—you just can't trust the buggers. Schools like the Bondurant School of High Performance Driving in Sonoma, California, which teach advanced evasive maneuvers, are strongly discouraged. It is too risky to let people with those kinds of abilities loose in everyday traffic. People should *not* know what it feels like to skid, how to set up for a turn at high speed, or how to make quick in-and-out moves while running a plastic-cone slalom.

Rebels Without A Cause

In fact, across the country, even your basic public-supported driver training has become suspect. And the fear of teaching someone how to manipulate the highways is most pronounced in the training of teenagers. Unlike the careful, appropriately terrified adult, someone such as Judy, your enthusiastic adolescent has a completely different air. Teenagers are naturally excitable, straining at the bit, eager for risks, so it is *you*, the driving instructor, who is afraid.

You have your hands full, and you are not going to get much help from the government or the school system. Driving courses that were once required in many high schools across these United States are now, in many cases, no more than elective courses. Unfortunately, one of the most important and practical skills, which, if properly taught, stresses community and interdependence, has been granted less importance in the curriculum than learning who blew up whom in what bloody war. The one course that is eagerly anticipated and enthusiastically participated in by almost all teenagers, driver ed is the one place where you really have even the worst, most rowdy student's attention, where that student can learn skills and attitudes that will spill over into all phases of his or her life, for his or her *entire* life, yet this is given backseat importance.

In car-happy California, for instance, driver training and driver education are merely electives, and the law requires only a minimum of six hours training behind the wheel to be eligible for a driver's license. In Japan, by contrast, driver's training assumes much more importance: the student must spend a minimum of seventeen hours learning to master a special training course replete with sloping road, sharp corners, difficult intersections— *plus* thirty hours learning auto mechanics, repair, and rules—just to get a provisional license. To qualify for a regular license takes from thirty to fifty hours of behind-the-wheel training.

But why this situation? Why the hesitation about extending proper driver training to teens in this country?

Some educators would say that learning a practical, integrative skill such as driving does not fit into the standard high school curriculum. The standard fare is a steady dose of testable and competitive academic courses and sports in which each person, considered solely as a separate entity, can be compared to a standardized scale and appraised in order (so the thinking goes) to allow society to operate.

But there are other arguments. The Insurance Institute for Highway Safety purports to show that driver's education in America kills five thousand humans a year by allowing teenagers access to our highways. Many authorities point out that adolescents are overconfident, high risk-takers, immune to their own mortality, and, statistically, are four times as likely as an adult to get in an accident.

Moreover, two influential long-range "scientific" studies of young drivers—one done in 1971 by the California Department of Motor Vehicles, the other the controversial De Kalb study, completed in 1983 under the auspices of the National Highway Traffic Safety Administration—assert that driver training does not, in any way, make for safer drivers.

Robert Terry, Highway Jeffersonian

As Zen Drivers, we certainly disagree with those studies, and feel they should be contested. In fact, they *have been* strongly contested by Robert Terry. Almost single-handedly, Terry was responsible for the (onetime) mandatory driver education and training programs in California's high schools. I spent one long, pleasant afternoon in Sacramento talking with Terry. Actually, I didn't do much talking, as Terry is a man wild with ideas and wisdom who talks nearly nonstop. Most of my time in Sacramento was spent trying to keep up with Terry as he tore through the halls in the Capitol Building, introducing me to one person after another, all the while going on about the miscreant state of driver education.

Terry proclaims himself an adherent of the Jeffersonian model of free and unfettered education, which should be the responsibility of the state. He calls the above studies flawed and tendentious, part of a "Delphic Process" that cannot possibly evaluate the importance of driver's training for each individual and society as a whole. His own work as director of the federally granted 1979 Task Force Study, launched to develop the definitive traffic safety education program, found that for a safety education program to be effective it would have to be a "cradle-to-the-grave process." In other words, one would have to analyze a lifetime's worth of driving experience and knowledge to come up with a statistically valid basis for an education program.

"We are trying to teach people how to survive in a mechanized society," says Terry. And so common sense alone should tell us that: one, driving is obviously a skill and should be amenable to the education process; and, two, since driver education/safety is obviously a lifetime process of accumulated experience, why not set the young driver in the right direction while you still have him or her at home, under the tutelage of both the high school system *and* the family system.

Toward this end, Terry has recently developed, in a growing majority of California's 375 school districts, what he calls a competency-based program of driver training. The program has two phases. The first phase, implemented to correct the random effectiveness of a mere six hours training behind the wheel, requires the high school student to become virtually *competent* at certain key driving maneuvers—navigating blind intersections, changing lanes effectively, entering traffic from a stop-parallel position, entering and exiting the freeway—before passing the course, whether this competence takes two hours or two hundred. The second phase involves the participation of the parents, and it was here, at the program's inauguration, that Terry met with the most skepticism from his peers. This phase entailed assembling the students' parents in a large auditorium and talking to them about driver education. It's hard enough to get a minority of parents involved in such things as the PTA—who would show up to hear a high school instructor lecture them about a meager elective subject? Well, as Terry tells it, that first experimental meeting was jam-packed and spilling over with concerned parents. Perhaps the school and legislative officials did not think driver training that important—but the parents did!

Terry encourages you as parents to participate in several ways. First and foremost you must complement driver training classes at home, especially the mechanical basics, such as steering, accelerating, and braking (those things our friend Judy learned in her first couple of outings). It's also important to create caring criteria for when and how your teenager drives: under what conditions they get their license (ability, grades. behavior, etc.), and under what conditions they get the keys to your car or their own car. (Remember your first car? I remember mine: a 1962 black VW bug. What a joy!) Parents' participation in their teenagers' driver education has fallen by the wayside, says Terry, which is a shame, because the involvement of the parents can really determine just how safely teenagers drive. This process is a wonderful opportunity to involve you in your adolescent's life; it's a way of showing love and concern, a way to share yourself. If you wait until your son or daughter is older before they learn to drive, you lose this opportunity. And down the road (pun intended) you would not have as good a driver. If nothing else, parents should take a hand in the driver education of their adolescents so those same adolescents as adults can keep alive the tradition of telling stories of their parents' undoings. Should I relate the tale of the time my father was teaching me how to drive over Malibu Canyon and after one particularly sharp turn screamed, "Stop the car! Just stop the car!" then got out, took five deep breaths, walked a circle around the car, got back in, and said, "Okay, continue"? Nah, I guess I won't.

On the Road Together

A parent's participation will determine how successfully his or her adolescent's natural driving abilities and talents will unfold. You, as a parent, are also the best one to help plant a sense of community in your son or daughter. This is exactly what Ed McSweeney, head of the San Francisco Unified School District's driver training program, wants to do; like Robert Terry, he wants to cultivate socialization. "I want to teach the kids and the instructors that we are all really working together to make the highways run safely," McSweeney told me one morning in his small bungalow office. *"I want them to know that driving is a social occasion."* In Zen Driving, this sense of oneness is what we hope to allow to unfold. For in reality we are not, and never were, separate from anything.

But, for teenagers, this is not an insight that comes easily. Nor, developmentally, is it suppose to come easily. (At least not according to modern psychologists.) Adolescence is an extremely tough time of life, complete with its own set of pressures and tensions, a make-it-or-break-it period centering on forging an identity. This is important to remember in working with your headstrong, defiant teenager on driving. Your attitude, of course, is crucial. For instance, instead of establishing yourself as an absolute authority, it would be much better to acknowledge the fact that you cannot teach them to drive, you can only allow them the space to learn. No doubt, it is your car, and they live under your roof, so you can say when he or she drives, and under what conditions they buy a car—but when you're playing their driving coach you should not say *how* they *should* drive. Again, it's a matter of allowing their innate ability to unfold naturally, at its own pace and manner. With a teenager this not only creates the awareness and experience necessary to be a safe, efficient, and happy driver, but also allows your teenager the room to develop his or her own identity. They want to be their *own* kind of driver, not a carbon copy of you (unless, perhaps, you're Mario Andretti). The two-pronged approach to Zen Driving is all you need relay: focus on being aware of everything around you. Driving is not a test; there's nothing moralistic about it, no right or wrong. Your apprentice is neither an ignoramus nor a genius. He or she is not a reflection or an extension of you. When a person is old enough to drive, he or she is old enough to be treated with the same respect with which you would treat anybody else.

Adolescence serves as a transition into the larger social network. Learning to drive becomes a *rite of passage*, a very real and important ritual symbolizing the transition into the wide world. And with you as their driving coach, the Zen non-method makes this process a whole lot easier and a lot less painful.

Sylvia

One of my most memorable challenges in working with a teenager is with Sylvia, age 16. It is memorable because although driving is for her an initation into the adult world, it isn't necessarily a passage into the bravado independence we sometimes prize too highly in this country. Sylvia and her parents moved here four years ago from another country, where community is valued more highly than individuality. Sylvia is a gifted musician, a pianist, and is also very shy. She went through driver education in high school here, passed her driver's test at the DMV, yet is having a hard time getting really situated behind the wheel. Confidence is hard in coming. Her parents are friends of mine, who one evening mentioned to me Sylvia's rather extreme diffidence when it comes to driving. They knew my ideas about Zen Driving, and my "driving experiments," as Sylvia's father called them, and asked if I would like to work with Sylvia? They, of course, knew I would say yes.

As I did with Judy, I first take Sylvia out to an abandoned parking lot, even though she already knows, mechanically, how to drive. In fact, she is an amazingly mindful, safe young driver. I set up an obstacle course of cones, and have her drive through them as she normally would, while I time her with my stopwatch. I make a game out of the practice, telling her to try and beat her previous time with every run. With three runs she does just that, shaving away a few seconds each time. The fourth and fifth runs, though, are about the same as the third. Her fear acts as a governor on her abilities, and she isn't about to go any faster. "That's perfectly fine," I tell her. "You've already shown a good margin of improvement, shown that you can be more assertive than before, by going faster the first few times. Now let's try and put that assertiveness to use in traffic."

My main task with Sylvia is to allow her to acknowledge her assertive capabilities herself. I know she is capable of taking more of an initiative in traffic, but if I simply tell her to do so, I'm doing nothing more than throwing up a rule that she'll follow just to please me, but will soon forget or avoid once she's on her own. By having her speed through the cones I got her to reflect on the fact that she is capable of going faster than she thought possible, but in actual traffic it is going to be a little harder to boost her confidence. And that is because she is such a conscientious, sensitive person. She is *too* polite. For instance, no matter who gets to the stop sign first, she always allows the other driver to go first. Sometimes she even smiles and waves at the other, often flabbergasted, driver. As for making a left turn at a green light against a stream of cars coming in the other direction, Sylvia notoriously aggravates drivers behind her by waiting for a regular ocean of a space between cars before turning. "You are a wonderful driver," I tell Sylvia, "you just need to drive in a little more New York state of mind."

One day when I know that Sylvia has to be home by 5:00 P.M. for her prized piano lessons, I devise a strategy to make her less self-conscious in traffic, to cause her to drive more assertively. Beginning at 3:30 in the afternoon, we drive through town, gradually working our way to the residential outskirts. After about forty-five minutes, Sylvia begins asking me the time, worrying about making it back. I continually tell her not to worry, that we'll be back in plenty of time. Actually, by 4:30, we are at a point where I know one must hurry to make it back to Sylvia's neighborhood by 5:00. Feigning disbelief, I tell her I've lost track of the time, and that she is going to have to drive faster than usual. Her first response is for me to drive, but I decline, assuring her that she can make it herself.

As we head back through town, I keep quiet, other than to apologize for losing track of the time. And the truth is, Sylvia does show more of an initiative, even venturing to make a right turn on a red light, after stopping, of course. I almost want to applaud, but I stifle my enthusiasm until we reach her home, only ten minutes late. "Like speeding through the cones," I tell her, "you are capable of driving more assertively. I simply wanted you to acknowledge that. And you drove just as safely as before, and, I think, you drove much more fluidly." She is a little mad at me, giving me a brusque, "Yes, thank you," before rushing up her front lawn.

I don't believe that creating a stressful experience to enhance one's education is the best method of instruction, but in Sylvia's case, I think the experience is valuable. In the future, I'm hoping that she'll be able to combine her natural assertive qualities with her already wonderfully established sense of community and politeness. When the two come together, without undue reflection, Sylvia may be the best Zen Driver of us all.

Jon

Now, let us switch gears, and consider cultures such as Los Angeles or Phoenix, areas almost completely dependent upon the automobile, where coming of age means sprouting not wings but four wheels, and where there dwells a particular variety of young driver whose fearlessness and temerity is quite legendary. These young people spend a great deal of time and energy testing the limits of their cars. Their cars are not only the focus of status and freedom—to be constantly cherried and tuned and pampered—their cars are first and foremost street performers, machines to be driven, and driven fast. They engage in street racing, dragging, Bonzai running, or just plain tearing around town. Driving behavior that, eventually, makes for excellent drivers. For those, of course, that live that long.

So far Jon, who I worked with for a couple of outings, has lived to age 19. He was a real challenge. Jon has three *very full* years of driving experience under his belt. He has also had his license suspended twice, including an arrest for excessive speed—over 100 mph (a felony). On our first outing, he sits arrogant and sulking behind the wheel, knowing, as I do, that in terms of pure, practical ability there is little he can learn. His awareness is as

finely tuned as his Firebird (which, on occasion, he guns to display his impatience), his
reflexes quick and sure. He also knows, as I
do, that were it not for the authority of his
father, he would not be here now.

As we begin traveling the suburban streets,
it is evident that Jon, though an accomplished
driver, is very full of himself. He drives like a
tiger prancing menacingly through the jun-
gle. He literally scowls and growls at other
drivers. It's nice to see that Jon has a strongly
established identity. But it would be nicer,
safer, more beneficial to him, if he could begin
to develop more of a democratic feeling for
his fellow drivers. I ask him how he feels, and
he replies that when he's "aboard," no one
can bug him or hassle him; he doesn't have to
worry about junk. Most of all, he adds after
some reflection, he feels respected. I nod, and
ask him if he could practice driving as a sort
of feeling experiment, to drive through the
streets respecting other drivers as much as he
himself feels respected. Also, since he can be
carefree, without worries, could he drive as
though no one around him, including his parents, boss, and other authorities in his life,
was bugging or hassling him. "Pretend you're
as confident and hassle-free as you say you
are," I tell him. "See how that makes you feel

about other drivers. Drive like that for a while." Jon, giving me a suspicious "this guy's nuts" look, continues driving through town. "Are you doing it?" I periodically ask. "Sure," Jon smiles. "Sure, I'm doing it, look at me, I'm doing it." He begins to laugh. "I don't know what the hell I'm supposed to be doing but I guess I'm doing it." And he sputters with laughter.

As we continue, it's obvious that Jon is growing more relaxed. As a result, his attention grows sharper and his driving more fluid. The second time I drive with Jon, he seems to enjoy himself a little more. He is no longer in a ready-to-tromp-on-it state of mind; he's a little more interconnected with his environment, including other drivers. I think his improvement stems from me just reminding him to take it easy, to remain mindful of others, to be a little more *sympathetic*. "It's not a me-versus-them thing on the road," I tell him. "Even in professional racing, you can bet that the winners never lose their synchronization with the cars around them. To consider the highway one whole, not a series of separate entities, makes driving a more intense and uplifting experience. That's what I mean by respect—to respect the whole picture, the whole shebang around you: people, cars, the road, you name it. That sort of respect puts you in a groove that will make you an even better driver."

"That makes some sense," says Jon, and I detect a slight note of sincerity. "But you better not mention racing to my father."

Quinton and Eda

Throughout the book, I've been talking about courting a higher awareness/experience of driving, of being in harmony with every moment of action around you, yet I don't mean that the practices of Zen Driving must be carried out only when you are alone in your car. You can certainly be a Zen Driver with passengers, as long as you don't allow them to distract you. A good Zen Driver feels perfectly comfortable with others in the car; in fact, just by the warmth of their company, if not by their light conversation, passengers put us more at ease, helping to free our mind of its incessant chatter, allowing awareness/experience a free and pleasant reign.

Quinton and Eda are a special case. Seldom do they drive alone—Eda never does—and they illustrate both the benefits and problems of driving with others. They are an elderly married couple, and have recently moved west from the east coast. Both have held valid driver's licenses for many years, yet both feel very uncomfortable driving the "foreign" and "insane" freeway grid and grind of Los Angeles traffic.

Driving with this couple, it's soon apparent what we need to work on. Quinton and Eda sustain themselves in traffic by keeping up a running commentary on just about every other driver on the road—they go too fast, they follow too close, they switch lanes too abruptly— negative comments that are, more often than not, spiced with speculations about where these drivers were born and where they are sure to go when they die. Quinton and Eda also constantly offer one another advice and directions, as if one was the pilot and the other the navigator. And meanwhile, as to their actual driving abilities, they drive hesitantly, with jerky, fitful motions, entirely devoid of confidence.

I ask them both for the duration of the session to try and turn off the criticism and maintain a quietness. I suggest that the one driving (Quinton goes first) simply focus single-mindedly on awareness, paying attention to, without judging, the road conditions as they unfold.

And along they drive—for a while. After about five minutes of stone silence, Quinton bursts out, "What should I do? Say something!"

"You're doing everything right," I say. "Just try and enjoy yourself," but Quinton balks. "How can I enjoy myself when I'm waiting for you to tell me what to do?" I explain to him and to Eda that you certainly do not need criticism or instruction from me on how to drive. What you need is to trust in your own decisions, to silently allow your natural driving abilities to take over. I explain that it's hard to maintain awareness and enjoy driving when you're constantly getting or expecting criticism from either yourself or others. All these thoughts get in the way; awareness is keeping your mind free of any content. It is also as much a physical as it is a mental sensation. If you focus on attention, if you're really looking, then you can feel how close you are to the center divider, you can feel how fast the guy behind you is gaining, you can feel a turn or the car next to you. But you need to be present! You don't need instruction, you need to look, constantly look!

I then practice an exercise with Quinton. Every once in a while I interrupt the silence by asking him what—without using the rearview mirror!—is behind him? Or, without turning his head, tell me what is on his left, or his right. "Are you going fast enough to keep up with traffic?" "What's the next freeway exit?" "Who got to this intersection first?" "What's behind you?" "What's on your right?" "How far ahead do you see?" A game is made of it, and slowly Quinton seems to understand that if he pays attention, if he keeps up his 360-degree moving picture and feels his way along the road and through traffic, he can answer these questions spontaneously. His awareness/experience is slowly beginning to become automatic.

While working with Quinton, I have not forgotten his other half. I know that Quinton and Eda have spent almost every minute of their adult lives together, and always will. Albeit mutually bossy, they're comfortable and utterly familiar with one another, be it at home, in the supermarket, or in the car. I can tell by the way they often complete one another's thoughts, or, to speak more directly to their driving behavior, the way they team up together against the "maniacs on the freeway." What I advise them to do is help one another trust more in their individual driving habits. Toward this end I have turned our driving sessions into something like Gestalt exercises. While Quinton practices his 360-degree awareness, I ask Eda to close her eyes, to remain quiet, and as we drive along, Quinton at the helm, to rate her anxiety on a scale from one to ten. I want Eda to feel—to experience—her anxiety, and thereby to gain control over it. This ranking her anxiety is kept up until Eda is finally able to let go and relax. Now she can open her eyes and fully watch her husband's driving. Things begin to go smoothly.

❀ When Eda herself takes the wheel, however, we're back to the old ways. The biggest anxiety for Eda is getting on the freeway. For this feat she relies completely on Quinton, who, the faithful navigator, looks around and tells her when to turn onto the onramp and when to merge into the freeway. In all fairness to Eda, she does every once in a while glance in her mirror, but for the most part she keeps her eyes straight ahead and merges when Quinton says merge. Suffice to say, this makes for an awfully unsmooth entrance, and a frightening ride. But once she's made it, Quinton congratulates her, and they share a sigh, as if they've just conquered some treacherous mountain peak.

Now, I want Eda to feel that sense of accomplishment based solely on her own efforts. Quinton is told to remain quiet (close his eyes and rate his anxiety if he has to) as I have Eda get on and off the freeway again and again on different onramps and offramps, each time asking her how she feels. "How does it feel to speed up?" "How does it feel to see the cars coming behind you in the mirror?" (I sneak a glance at Quinton, who, I could swear, is sitting there holding his breath, his face as red as a balloon.) "Is it better when you turn your head and look?" "Don't use the brakes to merge into traffic, rely solely on the accelerator pedal," I tell her. "What does that feel like? Does it make you fearful?" "You can do it yourself," I constantly assure her. As we continue, it's my hope that Eda will begin to acknowledge her own experiences of driving, instead of depending on Quinton for justification.

Individual and mutual trust is, of course, what I'm aiming for as I work with Quinton and Eda. For it's trust, gained only through the guidance of pure awareness and pure experience, that will make their driving sojourns on the L.A. freeways less hellish and more enjoyable, not to mention safer.

Zen Mind, Beginner's Mind

In Zen Driving it does not matter who you are, how old you are, or what your experience is—you are always beginning. Every time you venture out in your car, your driving experi-

ence should be brand new. Driving is old hat
only when you seem to be somewhere else. It
is enjoyable when you are really here, present
behind the wheel of your car, traveling
through the middle of the eternal moment.

FOUR

*The Fear
of Death
In a
Random
World*

*"What a long time
I have been running
after unrealities!"*

—*Jitoku Eki*

True Zen

It's rather difficult to pin down Zen—it's like trying to grab a handful of a rushing stream. "What is Zen?" asks Paul Reps. "Try if you wish. But Zen comes of itself. True Zen shows in everyday living, consciousness in action." What it is . . . is what it is: you and your car in motion down the busy road; "The thing in itself." It is much easier to define what is not Zen. And, appropriately, we have now come to the point where it's important to take a close look at what I have called "images of the UnZen," those fixed concepts, conditioned automatic response patterns (carp), and exigencies of personality that cloud our natural driving ability. Inundated by such images, we lose contact with our natural-self, we destroy the delicate balance of the driver-car-roadway system, and awareness/experience is left behind at the last rest stop, now replaced by anxiety, anger, uptightness, aggression, compulsion, and, of course, fear.

You're Going to Get Nailed

A recent radio commercial warns: "You aren't planning to be in an accident"—*loud screeching tires, horrendous crashing sounds*—"but it's always a possibility."

Of these unpropitious, unplanned events known as accidents, there are approximately 18,000,000 in America every year. They result in, on the average, 2,300,000 injuries and 45,000 deaths. Automobile accidents are, in fact, the leading cause of death for all Americans between the ages of five and thirty-five. But the really bad news, as the radio commercial asserts, is that cruising the nation's highways is like spinning the roulette wheel. *The California Driver Fact Book*, issued by that state's Department of Motor Vehicles, states categorically, "In a statistical sense, chance plays a major role in determining who is involved in traffic accidents." Craig Miller of the National Highway Safety Administration says, "It's probability, you're going to get nailed."

Wait, it gets worse.

According to psychologists who study driving, there are 1,500 psychomotor skills needed to drive a car. To many driving experts, this is simply too much for the poor driver to master. Our boggled experts discuss such things as "inherent human limitations on drivers' abilities," and maintain that "a certain magnitude of driver error for any driver must be considered normal." Normal! According to one insurance company study, the average driver makes 2½ errors for each mile of travel, so no matter how you look at it, haphazard driving habits must be considered commonplace. And all of this is borne out by studies that purportedly prove, yes, *statistically*, that formal driving education and training courses do not improve one's driving record.

Take all these numbers and rub them together and it doesn't look good. One's world view grows dim. If a drunk doesn't get you, or a fearless teenager, then you can be consoled by the happy fact that you are potentially doomed by your own innately flawed ability. We are victims of chance! Furthermore, no education or training system is going to save us. It's sad to say, but of all who dare to venture out in their cars, some, poor souls, never return. It's a dice shoot. And one day, in your case, it's just liable to roll up snake eyes. Bye-bye.

But hold on, don't go anywhere, it gets even worse.

The world is a dangerous, volatile place. Okay. But then there is human nature itself— the most reckless driver of all! Or so some say.

Power and Mastery

A few years back a driving researcher named L. Black did an interesting study. He interviewed a cross-section of motorists who agreed that cars should be designed with safety as their single most important feature. The motorists talked about various technical designs that would serve this purpose; for instance, they thought automatic seat belts were a wonderful idea. Overall, accidents made them very nervous indeed. Safety should come first—at least that is what they said.

Black then hypnotized each of these people, and the second set of interviews yielded quite different results. Safety was no longer the central issue. They now felt that a well-designed automobile was one that was sleek, low, and fast! Slow drivers were the ones who caused accidents. The hypnotized drivers now agreed that the greatest aspect of driving was the feeling of power and mastery of being behind the wheel!

This study is often cited to emphasize the dangerous tendencies bubbling in the unconscious of the average driver: wildness, excitement, unsatiable power, a vaunted sense of self. Sooner or later these powerful urges are going to ooze out, and out means out of control.

This interpretation belongs to that segment of psychology heavily influenced by Freud, and, as we know, the unconscious makes Freudians more than a wee bit nervous. This is because they see the world pretty much as an inhospitable place (tooth-and-claw, dog-eat-dog Darwinism). To them, we are beset by dangers from without and within; in fact, one is the reflection of the other. Only civilized society can save us. We must bend our natural inclinations (of power and mastery) in order to fit into the pleats of society; a draw is the best we can hope for. In theory, without that highway patrolman sitting there conspicuously at the side of the road—or at the side of your mind—our revved-up egos will press our accelerator pedals recklessly through the floor at every available chance.

We are as leery of black-and-white highway patrol cars as of black-and-white skunks. That is the idea of the authorities and many lawmakers: in order to keep us intact they need to play on our fears. Some years ago, along a hilly but open stretch of California highway, the authorities planted a life-sized wooden replica of a black-and-white patrol car behind an advertising billboard. Drivers instinctively slowed down when they saw the plywood imitation, even the veterans (like me) who regularly traveled this stretch of the road. If you want to control the highways, bank on fear— keep a cap on those dangerous inner drives.

Where the Wild Things Are

But is fear really what maintains the equilibrium of our highways? Are the highways really a primordial plain where wild beasts (including humans) roam about wantonly? All of this does nothing but reflect a mistrust of human nature. Fear is more a product of thought than reality, and a view that has never made much headway with Zen Buddhists. In Zen, fear as a deterrent of our wild inner drives is absurd. The inner, the unconscious, has a wisdom that can and should be followed. To tap into one's true personal power and mastery, whether in a car built for speed, or in one built for safety, is exactly the aim! It's tapping into natural-self!

Yet our culture, insecure and untrusting, seems to be constantly working against us. Warning: Fasten your seat belt! Warning: Drive defensively! Warning: Speed kills! Eventually, you begin to wonder: Is driving natural? Is an automobile, say your little Honda, or that sleek, dark green $40,000 Jaguar sitting over there in your neighbor's driveway, a product of Nature? Is this the way God planned it? If not, then perhaps many of the driving science experts are correct in positing "inherent human-to-vehicle limitations." When we climb into one of those iron, death-dealing devices, are we not removing ourselves from the natural world and entering a dangerous, artificial realm where screwing up must be expected?

If we allow ourselves to be brainwashed by a culture in love with dire statistics, then the answer is "yes." If we abandon our individual control, our belief in natural-self, and think of ourselves as a number in a future fact-book of auto-accidents, fear will take over our minds and bodies like a bad hangover. Such exaggerated fear is known as *anticipatory fear*—the fear of fear. It is this fear that cripples us, causing us, like stragglers in the herd, to fall victim to large predators. Drivers wracked by images of limitation and self-doubt develop a mind set that not only interferes with awareness and the dexterity needed to avoid a collision, but actually creates a kind of self-fulfilling prophecy: If you expect to hit something eventually, you eventually just might.

Through our fears we tend to bring about exactly that which we fear most. We attract large carnivorous car-eating beasties, and in their wake, profiting from it all, come the insurance companies. Under the influence of exaggerated emotions and delusions, we begin to rely on charms and talismans.

Trying to Ward Off Evil

It's important to note that insurance is purely a luxury item; if you can afford it, it protects you from scavenging lawyers and protects your monetary possessions. In the actual process of driving, however, insurance has no functional value whatsoever. At best, it's like those fuzzy dice you can hang from your rearview mirror: they don't do a thing but they look pretty dangling there. At worst, it can give you a false sense of guarantee—What, me worry, I'm insured—and it's entirely possible that such false assurances can cause you to let your awareness down, making you vulnerable to accidents. The writer Franz Kafka, who spent his entire adult life working for an insurance company, claimed that people buying insurance was like primitives trying to ward off evil. You cannot rely on medieval powers to protect you from accidents.

You need to rely on natural-self!

According to Webster's dictionary, there are two possible meanings of the word *accident*: "1) an unforeseen and unplanned event of circumstances; lack of intention or necessity: chance"; and "2) an unfortunate event resulting especially from carelessness or ignorance." Contrary to what you might believe, despite the fear of fate, the second definition best describes the reality on our highways in the vast majority of cases. It is the *only* definition accepted by Zen Drivers.

Do not be fooled by statistics. Insurance companies and organizations such as the National Safety Council and the National Highway Traffic Safety Administration deal out of necessity with large numbers. Statistics work well in predicting large-scale outcomes and calibrating profit margins, but they also create their own biases, and they don't measure the individual driver at all. You always want to remember the one about the statistician who drowned in a river that *averaged* two feet deep.

Fear and Fearlessness

The limitations on our driving abilities are, be assured, not a matter of statistics, but self-created and self-inflicted. When fear becomes a nagging inner instrument it deters our driving, and when we fall prey to the overcharged anxiety of anticipatory fear, we fall out of tune with the here-now of ourselves, our fellow drivers, and the highway system as a whole. Natural-self, the experience and awareness needed to handle *all* driving contingencies, never gets acknowledged, much less fully developed. Instead of driving in control of all situations, we fall hostage to them. In *California* magazine, Tom Huth relates a rather funny tale of a poor farmer literally frozen by fear. "Freeway aficionado and author Paul Pierce remembers a man he found one afternoon cowering on the center divider alongside his disabled car. He was a farmer who'd never taken the freeways before, and this was his sorry tale: He had entered into traffic in the left lane that morning with a full tank of gas, had been swept up helplessly into the race, been boxed in place by the other drivers, been afraid even to change lanes, had driven on in terror like this, always keeping to the left, being shuttled from freeway to freeway, for six hours, until finally he ran out of gas and coasted to a merciful stop against the fence."

There are dangers and things to fear, including fear itself, out there on the highways, but operating from natural-self we can easily handle them. Chogyam Trungpa tells us that "true fearlessness is not the reduction of fear, but going beyond fear. . . . In order to experience fearlessness, it is necessary to experience fear."

In Zen, fear is a perfectly natural, normal, and functional emotion, and like all healthy emotions, there are times for it to be switched on: tricky traffic situations that call for a steady dose of endocrines to boost our alertness, or emergency situations that call for a speedy rush of adrenaline to warn and ready the body/mind for immediate action. Fear helps us shift our awareness into another gear (suddenly it's raining; suddenly the freeway traffic ahead has to come to a dead halt), but just as we keep our foot off the clutch once we've shifted gears, there is no need to linger on fear. One need not dwell on the dangers of driving or constantly be reminded of them; fear is another one of those human traits that will assert itself quite naturally when the occasion arises. In short, you can trust the human system. It performs surprisingly well under all conditions, be it a sunny cruise under the big sky of Montana or a bumper-to-bumper grind through downtown Manhattan.

From Amoebas to Driving Machines

Driving, like everything else, has developed along the evolutionary scale. Over thousands of years humans have naturally adapted to various environments, from hot grassy savannahs to the modern city and high-speed transportation. Who, after all, can say that driving is not a naturally ingrained human activity, as much a part of the ecology as the species that created it? Who can possibly discriminate between what is nature and what is not? Is a tree natural and a house not? How about a bird nest? Were the first primitive tools of homo erectus a part of nature? As Zen Buddhism points out, pretending that all things are not interconnected and interrelated causes grave problems. You may prefer the feline jaguar that stalks the jungles of South America to the Jaguar manufactured by the British Motor Car Company, but you cannot say that one is more real or more natural than the other. Both evolved over long eons and both, for better or worse, are inextricably tied to their respective environments. There is certainly a cosmic thrill in seeing a live jaguar, but then there is definitely a thrill in driving a British Jaguar.

Specters of the Road

This unnatural notion that things are separate, this discriminating tendency of mind, this lack of faith and trust in human nature—in ourselves and others, these illusory images floating around like so many ghosts cause us to fear, to cling, to seek escape, to be overly aggressive, and, generally, to be uptight. The upshot is that we fall out of accord with natural-self and true personal power and mastery. And the more out of accord we become, the more powerful the specters that haunt our roadways.

Probably no place is as filled with these ghostly images of the UnZen as the city. The greatest trial for any driver is coursing through urban traffic, taking on one condition after the next, our patience, our clear mind, our intimations of harmony challenged at every turn. Here, in the city, frustrations can (if allowed) build to incredible crescendos, then clamor for release. City driving can turn even the most calm, good-natured driver into a raving misanthrope behind the wheel, or so you hear tell.

Mrs. Hyde

Sitting and talking with a bright, attractive woman one evening in Los Angeles, a graphic artist, as polite and charming as one can be, I'm amazed to watch, as she describes her daily routine of driving through the city to work, her transformation into a Mrs. Hyde of the roadways. It seems that Mrs. Hyde is not all that fond of her fellow drivers. She carries on the passenger seat a set of large cards in a homemade flip binder, flashing certain choice phrases at drivers making maneuvers that do not meet with her approval; "You Jerk, Move Over!" "Use Your Signal!" "Are You Blind!" are but a few of her signs. As extra arsenal, she carries a can of black spray paint. When someone parks next to her too tightly, causing her to struggle to get out, she leaves a wide black indelible streak on the offender's fender. However, Mrs. Hyde informs me, she is a good driver, and is only trying to survive alongside all the crazy drivers out there. (Further conversation turns up that this charming artist has been in three accidents in just the last year and has received "a few" moving citations.)

Road Rambos

The city's streets and expressways are not some sort of battlefield, or worse, some gaming field where personalities vie for righteous expression, yet, for many, that's the case. In their armored bubbles of moving territory, drivers often exhibit all manner of indecorous behavior (How many times are evil gestures thrown your way as you cross town?) they would never dream of using if walking. (If someone cuts in front of you on the sidewalk, or accidentally bumps into you, do you cuss at them or give them the finger as you walk away?) What motivates these "Road Rambos," as Martin Gottfried calls them in *Newsweek*? Why the "epidemic of auto macho—a competition perceived and expressed in driving"? Are people really that uptight and unhappy and unsure of themselves that they must act out their aggressions behind the wheel?

The answers to these questions, as we've already discussed, lie in the misconception that a person is separate from his or her ecology. A person clings to various opinions and prefabricated images when the connection to wholeness and acceptance is (in their minds) broken. A Road Rambo's ego/personality is always hanging out there in the wind, alone, aloof, exposed, and if you get too close to it, it feels threatened and denigrated. Ego then lashes out at its imagined persecutors. And if— God forbid!—Ego ever happens to be really threatened, if someone yells at Ego, or someone momentarily endangers Ego by making a bad driving move, why then Ego goes entirely berserk, all circuits beginning to fry. Those cars piloted by Road Rambos are not occupied by happy souls.

Not happy? Lord, some of them are downright dangerous!

Recently, along one of California's rural single-lane highways, a lone fellow in a pickup moved to pass another lone driver, but the second car wouldn't budge. Fine, thought the guy in the pickup, pulling a large caliber revolver from his glove compartment, opening fire on the offending driver. Little did he know that the other driver was also armed. Thus ensued a deadly game of highway leapfrogging, accompanied by a gun battle. For miles the two shot it out, reloaded, shot, fired again. Finally an amazed driver phoned the highway patrol, who set up a roadblock and captured the dueling drivers.

It's wild, it's woolly, and it's very weird. But such runaway aggressiveness is the natural consequence of egotism and the false notion of separateness. In drivers who reach for their revolvers, some horrible threshold has obviously been crossed. In 1987 there were approximately one hundred shooting incidents on U.S. highways, with southern California leading the way. We shouldn't be too surprised, however, at the murderous thoughts coursing through drivers' heads. An early

1970s study of drivers in Salt Lake City revealed that twelve percent of the men and eighteen percent of the women would gladly knock off certain drivers if they could. "It's nothing new," said California highway patrolman Ken Daily to the Los Angeles *Times* about drivers wanting to kill their neighbors on the road, "it's just that now they have weapons." As if a fast-moving, multiton hunk of metal wasn't enough of a weapon, drivers now have—and use!—loaded firearms.

But once someone is fragmented from his or her environment, from the road and the others on it, he or she become potential road warriors. Drivers often feel the road is their own, and do not kindly tolerate challenges to their territory. Raymond Novaco, a professor at the University of California at Irvine who studies freeway stress and anger, says drivers live in their own "private bubbles," and once those bubbles are broken, out comes "Mr. Hyde." Also, drivers who feel disconnected from their awareness and experience feel they are anonymous—another factor behind the shootings. Dr. Ange Lobue of College Hospital, (Cerritos, California), an expert on driving stress, says that driving can be like war. "You can kill because you don't know your adversary," he says.

So take your potential road warriors and put them anywhere on the 525 miles of L.A. freeways at rush hour, 470 miles of which are going to be congested, where the average speed is 18 mph, and you have an explosive mix. It's not a good sign when you live in a city where you can call the highway *shooting line*.

An Impartial Participant

How can we avoid becoming uptight driving monsters and angry Road Rambos? What can we do with anger and frustration when they come sneaking up on us in our rearview mirror?

When confronting any driving situation, you do not want to react aggressively out of ego (the "me-versus-them" theory of driving), nor do you want to be a passive victim of fate and chance. "The basic difference between an ordinary man and a warrior," Don Juan tells Castaneda, "is that a warrior takes everything as a challenge, while an ordinary unaware man takes everything either as a blessing or a curse." What you want is to have no *personal investment* in any aspect of driving. No ego-ness, no victim-ness, no mind, no form, no thought, no image-attachments of any kind. "Everything that happens, and above all, what happens to me, should be observed impartially, as though on the deepest level it did not concern me," writes Herrigel. To drive from a place of pure, impartial awareness/experience divested of any sense of separate "me" is to cut off at the source any sour feelings for our fellow drivers. To rely solely on awareness and experience is to rise above every shot at our emotions from others—to be beyond petty grievances both inside and outside of ourselves. Centered in awareness/experience, traffic flows around you, and you move along as in a natural slipstream.

So now, driving along, you're suddenly startled by this high-speed, high-performance machine that comes flying out of nowhere and, within a hair's breath, deftly zips around you. It doesn't cause you to swerve or break, but still, as you watch it disappear into the horizon, how do you react? If you have any reaction at all you are not driving from pure awareness/experience. Consider, again, that there is no territory you need to protect, no ego that need be offended, no value system that calls for an emotional judgment. So, what's to react to? Some fancy little car flitted by you like a bug; you're aware of that, you experience the car whizzing past, and *that's all*!

The Sound of Aggravation

We need to accept things as we find them and as they come. This allows us to flow with traffic and to assert our skills when needed. Any other approach is setting ourselves up for aggravation.

An aggravated driver is one who has fallen from grace with the highways. Easily identifiable, these individuals are the ones who like to emit loud, shrill, obnoxious sounds by leaning indiscriminately on their horns, sounds that always remind me of a fellow I knew named Dale.

I will only tell one story (there are many) about Dale, this husky, friendly (except for his explosive temper), likable, and bear-like person. It seems there was one thing that Dale absolutely could not tolerate, that offended him to the core of his being, and that was horns. One day, a car that was giving Dale fits stalled on him in the right lane of a four-lane street in Santa Monica. He got out, opened the hood and searched for the problem. He hadn't been there but a minute when a fellow in a Corvette pulled up behind him and began blaring his horn. Dale peeked around his hood at the Corvette, only to hear another obstreperous blast! "Couldn't he tell the hood was open and I was having trouble?" Dale asked me over the phone from U.C.L.A. Hospital. He was there at the emergency room with the police waiting to see if the guy from the Corvette would regain consciousness. Would I be able to meet him at the police station later and bail him out?

Perhaps Dale would have fared better in Denmark, where horns are outlawed. Even in this country, there are many people, usually folks with aging cars and rusted horns, or people like Dale who yank the horn wires of every car they own, who have driven accident and hassle-free for many years without the "protection" and anger-venting convenience of a horn. The fact is, in Zen Driving, if we're truly aware of the surroundings of which we are a part, we do not need a horn. In Zen Driving, if someone does something unthoughtful or breaks the highway guidelines and puts us at temporary risk, our job is to avoid a collision and get on down the road calmly, not to voice our anger or fear with our horn. Contrary to what some people might believe, honking does not teach the other driver a lesson. It does not wake them up. It only serves to get them more uptight or more fearful or more sleepy and withdrawn from their environment. Our behavior, if divisive and angry and righteous, can only breed like behavior and perpetuate the problem. Besides, to travel from here to there without blaring out a negative emotion on our horn makes for a more uplifting drive.

Furthermore, wonderful folks everywhere, like Dale, will salute and thank you.

Just More Carp

The proclivity to lose one's temper is just another conditioned automatic response pattern, an ugly carp we get attached to, often against our will. Otherwise known as compulsions or addictions, these attachments are extraneous dependencies that we use to complete something in ourselves we *assume* to be lacking, or to handle something we *imagine* we cannot handle. Such compulsions and addictions are, in essence, a forgetting of natural-self.

In driving, the greatest lapse of memory centers around the use of alcohol and other drugs while on the road. This particular carp is singularly responsible for half of all the nasty things (i.e., dead and mangled human bodies) that can possibly happen while driving. People who insist on drinking or using drugs while driving should have as warnings bumper stickers that read "I brake for hallucinations," and little yellow signs hung in their windows that say "No One On Board." To put it succinctly, we cannot possibly practice Zen and good driving while intoxicated or allowing some weird chemical to go coursing through our system. Studies, physiology, and common sense support the harmful effects of drugs on driving—as everyone well knows. The enlightenment of Zen is the result of discipline and practice. Alcohol, tobacco, cocaine, marijuana, and all the rest are very deceptive imitations. If you can't get high on just plain driving, just plain don't drive. Amen.

Also, we need to stay aware that, as clean as we may be, some of our fellow members of the highway do, in fact, abuse drink and drugs. We cannot forget that they too are part of the transportation ecosystem. It is up to us to drive carefully around them, to avoid excuses like, "The dude was all over the road, I had'a swerve a buncha times before I finally hit him."

Driving With the Sandman

Richard Baker, former abbot of the San Francisco Zen Center, once said that at *no time* should a person not be as fully aware as possible. The absolute clarity achieved during meditation should be with a person every moment of his or her life. In driving, without exception, this must hold true. And yet if we are

preoccupied with images or foreign sub-
stances or oddball habits, our awareness sputters and lags and we end up, more or less,
asleep at the wheel. We, at times, literally forget where we are.

A young engineer I once knew was traveling
the open highway, trekking across the sage-
brush of Utah. He had just picked up a new
motorhome for his company in Salt Lake City
and was taking a short holiday by delivering
it to Los Angeles. He sat in the comfortable
driver's seat, hands on the wheel, feet up on
the dash, switched to cruise control. Listening
to the stereo, drinking a Coke, he felt like he
was in his own cozy living room back home.
His mind wandered across a thousand things.
And when he finished his Coke, he got up and
casually walked toward the back of the van to
the refrigerator to get another one. He said he
got about halfway down the aisle when a horrible thought intruded upon him: *Who was
driving?* He was able to dash back to his seat
and dive behind the wheel before the motorhome veered off the highway.

There are different ways to lose awareness
behind the wheel. You can forget you're driving, you can also push past all human limits
and drive your car or truck right into another
dimension—the dimension of dreams. A pro-

fessional cross-country driver once described to me what that is like: "You pride yourself on the fact that it's impossible for you to fall asleep at the wheel. No way are your eyes gonna droop or your head tip. You hold yourself rigid, and the sleepier you get, the more you force your gaze ahead down that damn road. And then what happens is that you're concentrating so hard on the road and the scene ahead, it becomes fixed. The whole road scene then becomes like a take-off for a fantasy or a daydream. Like in a movie, the road scene just slowly dissolves into the next scene, only this next scene is totally inside your head. Without you realizing what's happened, you're asleep, dreaming."

In the old days when a driver got sleepy, he'd pull over to the side of the road, get out, fold open the hood to the engine, and grab the electric coil. (Good morning!) In a Zen monastery meditation hall, during *zazen* (meditation) one monk will be assigned the task of slowly walking about the hall with a flat, tapering piece of wood known as a *keisaku*. His job is to rap the shoulder of any monk who is slumping or has fallen asleep.

Shy of electrocuting yourself or being snapped into awareness by a whack on the shoulder blades, how do you stay alert while driving? Like most things, maintaining the ongoing high awareness referred to by Zen is a matter of practice, and eventually, as a result of practice, such awareness will become both enjoyable and second nature. You will recognize that you *are* awareness. You will also recognize that when awareness becomes too much of a chore, it's time for a rest. The practice of Zen has often been stated as, "When hungry, eat, when tired, sleep." When the Sandman crawls into the driver's seat with you, whether he comes in the form of drowsiness, or he causes you to be overcome with emotions, obsessed with thoughts, or just suddenly gives you the urge to walk to the back of your vehicle for another soft drink, it's a good idea to be aware of him. If you can't convince him to leave, then why not just pull over to the side of the road and stop. Take a cat nap, beat your fists on the dashboard, have a cold drink, do what you need to do until you get that wonderful desire to drive again.

Maya

Basically, this chapter has been about driving while unaware or unconscious. Rather than facing things as they really are, rather than driving from the pure awareness and experience that is our natural, God-given natural-self, rather than using a discipline such as Moving Meditation to put us in touch with this ability so that we may practice using it, we cling to a vast accumulation of conditioned *stuff*: our imagined fears, our thoughts of inadequacy, our thoughts of how it should be, our images of who we are (personality), our untrusting world view, our reliance on external controls, our uptightness and anger and aggression, our desire to escape and ingest strange chemicals, and our general somnolence. In short, we indulge in illusions (maya). These illusions, these image-attachments, have been amassed over a lifetime of conditioning and learning, and we retain them, calling them knowledge, a sense of self, our way of relating to the world. We cling to them, we hang on, as to the tail of a tiger, and we dare not let go, for fear that they all might turn around and devour us.

The monk Chikan from Kyogen was a prideful man whose analytical abilities and knowledge of the sutras was unequaled. One day Chikan was approached by his teacher, the Zen Master Osho. The Master complimented Chikan on his intellectual prowess, then said to him, "The matter of birth and death is the most fundamental of all. Without telling me what you've learned from your readings, give me an essential word about your Self before you came out of your mother's womb. Answer me quickly!''

Chikan stood before him silent and dumb-founded.

 For weeks Chikan flipped wildly through all of his books and returned time after time to Osho with one answer after the other, all of which were rejected as wrong. Frustrated and exhausted, Chikan entreated Osho to give him the answer. "No," the Master said, "you cannot attain it from outside yourself. And even if I did tell you a word about it, it would be from my experience and understanding and not yours.''

Chikan lost all trust in himself, and so thoroughly disgusted with himself was he that he burned all his books and left the monastery, vowing to give up his study of Zen Buddhism. He slunk off into the forest angry and uptight. Eventually he took up an isolated existence living in a ruined temple far from everything and everyone. Here he lived, but not in peace, for Osho's question continually haunted him.

Then one day, while he was sweeping, he happened to brush aside a small shard of tile, which hit a bamboo stock, making an odd, unfamiliar sound. Startled by this unexpected sound, Chikan suddenly awakened to his true Self. He burst out laughing, then sat down and wrote out a short verse:

> The sound of something struck,
> and I forgot everything I knew.

FIVE

*On the Road
as a
Zen Driver*

*"How boundless and free
is the sky of Samadhi!"*

—Hakuin

Samadhi

Now we're ready to put our Zenfulness through the paces. We're ready to explore the Zen Driving experience under all conditions, no matter what our mood or current life predicament: whether we're driving a junker or a dream machine, whether it's snowing or the sun's shining, whether we're chugalugging through city traffic, gliding along the freeways, or cruising the open highway. On the road as a Zen Driver, every encounter is a full and an immediate one.

Now, having kept our awareness and experience of driving at a sensitive pitch, we have shed those ungainly images of the UnZen that had previously bogged us down. Each moment comes now like a haiku poem, "devoid," as R.H. Blyth says, "of all our mental twisting and emotional discoloration." No matter what detours the road, or our mind, throws up at us, we are in a position to remain unflappable.

We drive from a state the Zen masters call "potent emptiness": no thought, no mind, no form. Yet we are full. Our minds are never stuck in any one place; every road sign, pedestrian or Porsche strikes us as a sight unseen. We are in a state of *samadhi*, a Sanskrit word that means "concentration, the quality of meditation," a state that cannot be described, only experienced.

Nevertheless, let me *try* to describe it; that is, describe the experience of it. I raced motorcycles (motocross) for six years when I was younger, and was pretty good, advancing to the expert class. A friend recently asked me how I got to be good, how I got to be faster than the majority of competitors. I was thrilled at the question, for I loved the opportunity to talk about racing, but realized, as I was talking, that actually I didn't have the slightest idea how I got to be good. The more I thought about it, the less I could put my finger on the reason or reasons. The fact is, I just practiced and raced all the time, and gradually I grew more confident, smoother, and faster. Everyone knows the techniques that will make him faster—braking deeper into the turns, accelerating faster out of them, using the correct body english to improve traction—but only a few transcend these rules in action, and really there is no describing how that is done. It is a matter of assertion, but that assertion must grow spontaneously out of practice. There were always guys more assertive, more fearless than I, but they always seemed to be the ones who spent the most time in the pits, or on crutches. When I raced I performed in a state of *samadhi*. But only now, in hindsight, do I know that.

The Big City, Honey

Other than racing, the greatest challenge to any driver's *samadhi* arises, without a doubt, while he or she is venturing through the clamorous city. It's a trial because driving through the city is not something we usually do for pleasure. ("Honey, get the kids, we're going for a drive through rush-hour traffic.") Most of us drive through the city on our way to work or to run errands. We usually have a destination firmly planted in mind; before we leave our driveways our heads are predictably filled with expectations, dread, or blind resignation.

The Zen Driver, of course, will not leave his or her driveway in such a state of mind. It only takes a few moments of reflection to quiet the expectations and diffuse the dread. As Zen Drivers, we're quite aware that as we roll through city traffic our patience and harmony will be impinged upon at every turn. Here in the city we must constantly accommodate the changing conditions and shifting rhythms, stop and go, fast and slow; we can't allow our peace of mind to settle too comfortably into any one pace or tempo. Within the city arena we know we will be forced to make at least two hundred decisions a mile: red light, green light, left turn on arrow only, bus lane only, one-way street ahead, no right turn on signal, siren—pull over, while all the while we're surrounded by other cars, buses, trucks, motorcycles, bicycles, pedestrians, joggers, and stray dogs. Obliged to process a world of signs, instructions and human behavior at every second, our minds are running at high RPM.

In this maelstrom, more than ever, we must find our immovable wisdom and trust in awareness and experience. Being a Zen Driver in the city, in fact, may be the most rewarding encounter of all. If we maintain a Zen mind amid the city's hundreds of impulses, but for a short trip through traffic, we will emerge from our car bristling with life.

Retaining a Zen mind within the city's canvas of everchanging sights and circumstances means being centered in that pure sense of personal power and confidence borne of single-minded awareness/experience. That means being in it but not of it. "When a person's sense of inner achievement has become muted," says Tanouye Tenshin, "he turns to the clamor of the world. Losing all sense of a living center, he is caught in the bondage of a hundred different situations." Crash! Lose your inner sense of confidence and you fall from natural, spontaneous driving ability and end up being emotionally *and* physically tossed about by your surroundings.

But if we are centered in awareness/experience, city traffic flows around us, and we move along as in a natural slipstream. We accept things as we find them. The urban environment becomes a place of varying movements and cadences, which we respond to with our own inner sense of resonance. The only way to handle an unexpected delay, for example, is to feel connected to the whole ongoing show. It's not just my delay, it's a snag in the whole works, calling for us to sit there and quietly shift to a different inner rhythm. We need to steer clear of anticipation—we cannot *not* expect traffic jams, we cannot *not* expect to be cut off at times. There's simply no need to rush, because when we do our minds freeze in anticipation of our destination and we remove ourselves from the here-now and our awareness grows murky. Even if we do lose a minute or two by driving calmly in the flow (or snag) of traffic, we will more than make up for our time by arriving at our destination not at the stressed end of our rope, but alert, at ease, attuned. And as for those Road Rambos and those drivers who make stupid mistakes, we merely factor them in, and calmly drive around them.

Honey,
I Twisted
Through More
Damn Traffic
Today
—from a graphic work
by Edward Ruscha

It's hard to reiterate how important and how difficult this task is for the city driver. The city truly is a test of a Zen Driver's mettle and mindfulness; yet if we can remain unflappable and not get upset and flustered by the many potential aggravations thrown at us by the city's byways, if we can stay in pure awareness/experience, in *samadhi*, then this accomplishment is absolutely guaranteed to make us feel good. Skillful, peaceful city driving is the Zen Driver's crowning achievement. It's our Zen initiation, our entrance (no toll), of which in Zen there are many, to the *great path.*

The Freeway

The great path has no gates,
Thousands of roads enter it.
When one passes through
    this gateless gate
He walks freely between
    heaven and earth.

—Mumon

Navigating the city's streets is a test of our Zenfulness. One has to work at it. The relief and the reward, however, come when we gain access to the city's freeways and expressways. Then, as if charmed, we slip into a simple pleasure and harmony. Natural-self is given full rein. A big green highway sign says, "No Mind Ahead, Use High Gears," and all of a sudden we're operating freely between heaven and earth.

Really, there's nothing more beautiful, and it has such a nice name: freeway. A broad twelve-lane swath of glistening cement snaking into and over the horizon. It is pure suchness! Accelerating up the onramp, catching the main current and letting it carry us down the flow of speeding automobiles, we are gliding down the sight of endless white lines, long gently banking curves, under and above the streets, drifting past lofty buildings, cutting a deep wide fissure through the dense city.

The really wonderful thing is it's difficult to tell where one ends and the rest of the drivers begin. The stream of cars washes down the freeway as one fluid body. Here, as at no other time, we absolutely let go into the One. We ease into a new, more soothing rhythm, our awareness widens (from being a one-celled organism to a multicelled creature) and our driving experience . . . well, to find yourself in a small niche, at high speed, with cars all around you is certainly quite an experience! It's the actual *feeling* and *sensation* of being something bigger than oneself. It is an experience that, if we thought about it—like watching a large flock of blackbirds dipping and turning in the air as one black-speckled cloud, each bird in perfect formation—we could not figure out how it's done. All we know is that it's done by letting go, by non-action; without thinking about it, without losing our individuality, we are interconnected with the Whole. We are driving along freely between heaven and earth.

But it's a delicate balance. The simplest thing can often interrupt this freeway flow.

In Los Angeles, a beautiful woman fixing a flat in the emergency lane is enough to back up morning traffic for miles. An overpass, at certain traffic densities, causes just enough of a minute hesitation in the drivers' consciousness that forward progress can be stopped. Too sharp a curve has the same effect. Individual drivers who fall out of synchronization by making lane changes too abruptly or too slowly, who follow at too long a distance, who merge in a sloppy manner, or who don't plan their exit properly— these drivers can gum up the works very quickly. And, of course, there's just so much room aboard the freeway snake: too many drivers crowding their One, and the One becomes the Many-At-A-Dead-Stop. Back we go to processing our feelings in a mindful way.

Back we go to our own inner balance, a balance that is anything but delicate, a balance that once we tap into we never lose. It never comes to a dead standstill. It is this inner equilibrium that allows us to resonate with our environment; it allows us to adapt to any situation, without giving up our individual integrity. In this sense, any way we go is a freeway. In essence, there is little difference between city driving and freeway driving. There are just different rhythms, different songs.

Good Vibrations

Once on the Zen-way, if we are attuned to the varying traffic situations as we find them, driving sometimes feels just like dancing, and just as music is the perfect complement of dancing, so can it also be for driving. Motion and music seem to harmonize well.

Music, whether rollicking guitars or a melodious waltz, invites us into the here-now by muting our chattering brains and amplifying the singularly natural rhythms of driving. Tunes in our cars help restore us to our natural selves. As we tune it in and turn it up, we slip into a more alive frame of mind.

> Now some guys they just give up living
> And start dying little by little piece
> by piece
> Other guys come home from work and
> wash up
> And go racing in the streets
> —Bruce Springsteen

Our performances in all aspects of our lives are heightened when they become second nature to us. Music helps us achieve that spontaneous state. Think, for example, of construction workers welding girders fifty stories high with their portable stereos blaring by their sides. Music augments the natural rhythms of actions like driving by putting us further in touch with our experiences.

Actually, music may be only an escort into the deeper audible pleasures of driving. For one of the most wonderful experiences of relatively long-range driving is that after listening to music for so many miles, the actual meter and rhyme of the car, the road, the scenery, become more serene and meaningful *in silence.* After all, the speed and motion and sound of the car creates its own natural rhythm which, like music, like the rhythm generated by chanting a mantra while meditating, filters out noisy thoughts and feelings and is conducive to high arousal and awareness. Put simply, driving can be a very enjoyable pastime: just as good as turning on your stereo at home and easing back into your soft couch. A new perception peeks through.

Cross-Country Riffs

Surely one of the loveliest unpronounced melodies is cross-country driving. As part of the desert landscape, wide vistas, and a blue-white sky, heat waves rising off the shimmering black highway, we find ourselves, in the words of Robert Penn Warren, "whipping on into the dazzle." Sailing on down the road in our precision machines, country music waltzing from our radios, cross-country driving grants us the powerful sense of driving as an act that flows spontaneously from our natural-self. In such fine attunement "remarkable things happen," writes Robert Pirsig in *Zen and the Art of Motorcycle Maintenance*, "and you go flying across the countryside under a power that could be called magic."

But the dazzle and the magic can suddenly flag and fizzle if, while zooming across the landscape, your machine suddenly decides to break down. The music dies as you drift to a dead stop in the soft, sandy shoulder.

For one such as myself, who tends to drive older, used cars, this is not an altogether uncommon occurrence. Once, in southern Utah, I found myself on the side of a baking desert road with a leaking water pump and an overheated engine. At moments like this, one's Zenfulness gets strained to the outer limits. You begin to wonder: Are the Fates against me?

Junkers and Dream Machines

Robert Pirsig writes of the differences between himself, who rides an old motorcycle and constantly works on it on his cross-country journey (his vision quest), and his traveling companion, John, who rides a brand new motorcycle and would rather not know what a spark plug does. Pirsig maintains that his familiarity with the engineering of his machine grants him a sense of control over his fate. John, on the other hand, "looks at the motorcycle and he sees steel in various shapes and has negative feelings about these steel shapes and turns off the whole thing."

Our sense of Zen Wholeness, the interconnectedness of the car-driver-road ecosystem, is obviously broken if we rule out the car itself. When you drive an old junker, and you aren't exactly dining out with the Gettys every night, you probably work on your car yourself. And you find that when you change the oil, or adjust the timing, or change the clutch, you end up feeling pretty good about your accomplishment. There is a little part of you in the machinery. But even if you've never had greasy hands in your life, it's a good idea to remain aware of the inner workings and the fine engineering that propels you down the road.

In short, the more in touch we are with our cars, the less we take for granted, and the better Zen Drivers we become. Even if we have only the most rudimentary awareness of the combustion engine and the drive-train, whether we achieve that awareness by working on our cars ourselves or by sitting regally and starry-eyed in the plush new leather upholstery of our dream machines daydreaming of how it all works, the more power that can be called magic we have at our disposal.

As one who has spent many an hour studying repair manuals and turning wrenches, I can attest to that ''magic.'' It's the satisfaction that comes from feeling responsible and mindful of our own auto fortune. Believe me, it makes a great deal of difference, especially when you're sitting in ninety-degree heat with a busted water pump. It's what cools you down so that *you* don't overheat and blow a mental gasket. (Once, an eccentric friend of mine broke down on Topanga Canyon Blvd., and before I could get to him, he had flipped out, had, in fact, tossed every tool in his trunk into the bushes, except a hammer, which, when I got there, he had in both hands, threatening to smash his hood.) You either march to the nearest phone and calmly call your friendly AAA people, or you do as I did, which was to hitchhike to the nearest town, buy a new water pump, return to my car and install it. With a sense of achievement, my *samadhi* unbroken, I resumed by trip: Me and Robert Pirsig, attuned to the music of the old Zen Highway.

Neither Rain, Nor Sleet, Nor Snow . . .

But even the effortless melody of cross-country driving can segue into other, shifting rhythms—all according to the weather.

Los Angelenos often boast of being the best drivers in the world. Maybe so. Yet it's interesting and not a little amusing to watch what happens when it rains in L.A. These same expert drivers are suddenly skidding and crashing into one another with alarming frequency. The rain baffles them. (And God help them if it ever snowed.)

To be a driver for all seasons, we need to be a seasoned driver. We need experience driving in various weather conditions. Rain, snow, sleet, fog, high winds, dust storms, ice, hail, tornados, volcanos, earthquakes, the end of the world—there's no reason why we can't respond to any change in the weather, there's no reason why we can't enjoy driving under any cloud pattern. But experience is the key, the only key.

We need practice, and a lot of it, for driving in different weather. Our powers of awareness/experience must be tuned to the highest notch, translatable to any road condition, for our car is going to feel different in different conditions. We need a high awareness of that feel. Being told that if you get into a skid you should turn your steering wheel into the direction of the skid means little if you've never been in a skid before. Only drivers who have experienced a loss of traction can really respond effectively if it happens again. The same is true of braking in the snow, driving in fog, hydroplaning in the rain. So what can we do? Short of studying the weather section in the morning paper to find a rainy or snowy section of the state to practice sliding across the road on (not a good idea), we must simply remain acutely aware of how differently our car handles in various weather conditions.

After all, there really is no such thing as inclement weather. There are sunny days, there are rainy days, there are foggy days. No day is better or worse than the other. We can't drive a wet road the same as we do a dry one, so why compare them? A snow-covered road is not a slippery summer road. A snow-covered road is a snow-covered road. In Zen Driving we are not locked into driving any one way under any one road condition, nor are we deceived by the cozy temperature-controlled interior of our car. We remain as connected with the outside weather as though we were on foot.

Once we've gained the requisite experience and awareness, we can acclimate to any weather condition. Then, no matter what the road condition or climate, our only concern is the weather inside our head.

> In spring, hundreds of flowers;
> in autumn, a harvest moon;
> In summer, a refreshing breeze;
> in winter, snow will accompany you.
> If useless things do not hang in your mind,
> any season is a good season for you.
>
> —Mumon

The Everyday World

We all know that, if we allow them, our moods and life situations can affect our driving. (For example, studies show that people going through a divorce have a higher accident rate.) But no matter what the situation, inner or outer, if we remain ourselves, our natural-selves, then we can weather any storm. During excessively rough times, rough weather or rough traffic, when our awareness/experience seems to be drooping, we can always shore it up by practicing Moving Meditation.

If we remain aware, experiencing situations as they roll by, driving eventually becomes not only a means to a specific destination, but a means to put us in fuller touch with whatever we do. Once empowered and attuned to the old Zen Highway, it's just a short cruise to a sense of power and mastery in our walking world. In this sense driving is like *kinhin*. In formal Zen meditation halls, *zazen* (sitting meditation) is intermittently broken by *kinhin*, short periods of walking meditation. As Roshi Aitken put it, "*Kinhin* is, we may say, halfway between the quality of attention demanded by sitting meditation and the quality of attention demanded in the everyday world."

So finally we park, and leaving our car behind (it can sit and meditate on its own for a while), we enter the everyday walking world with that centered, high-attentive sense of natural-self achieved while driving. We've carefully stuck it in our pocket along with our car keys. But nothing has really changed as we leave our car for our next activity. Our natural-self is always with us. (Where else could it go?) As the old adage says, "Wherever you go, there you are."

The Zen Mind
The Zen Mind is reflected in whatever we do. Each moment, each happening, is an opportunity to further ourselves, to enjoy our lives, *if* we approach each moment and each

happening from a full-involvement state of
Zen Mind, in natural-self, free of image-attachments and dualistic thoughts. This practice, which we gained as Zen Drivers, gives
special meaning to our everyday affairs; it lifts
them to a new level of enlightened enjoyment
and participation. "Far from being incompat-
ible with the requirements of everyday life,"
writes Robert Linssen in *Zen Buddhism and
Everyday Life*, "Zen confers on it its own full
revealing value. There are no actions which
we should consider as 'ordinary' in contrast to
others which we regard as 'exceptional' or extraordinary. Zen asks us to bring to bear the
intensity of an extraordinary attention in the
midst of all so-called 'ordinary' circumstances." Linssen insists that each incident of
daily life can be an occasion for *samadhi* and
enlightenment.

This includes all those things waiting for us
at the end of our drive, from relationships to
baseball games, but especially that most
dreaded of events—more often than not our
driving destination: work. Roshi Philip Kapleau, like other Zen advocates, sees everyday
affairs, most notably work, as (once again) an
opportunity to achieve a fuller realization and
enjoyment of natural-self. "If work is to serve
this function," Kapleau points out, "workers

must train themselves not to evaluate their
jobs as boring or pleasurable, for one can only
make such judgments by 'stepping back,' thus
separating himself from his work. They must
learn to relate to their jobs single-mindedly,
with nothing held back—in other words, with
no 'thought gaps' between themselves and
their work. Performed this way, work acts as

a cleanser, flushing away random, irrelevant
thoughts, which are as polluting to the mind
as physical contaminants are to the body. Thus
work becomes, like everything else, an expression of True-mind, creative and energizing. This is the true nobility of labor. To work
this way is called in Zen working for oneself.''

From a Zen point of view we all work for
ourselves, each of us finding his or her particular road to . . . to whatever we feel worth-
while pursuing, be it the enlightenment of a
simple lifestyle in the country, or the enlightenment of an ambitious project like uncover-
ing a new particle in physics. Moving
Meditation, which teaches us the pure aware-
ness/experience of *samadhi*, *literally* moves
us down this road, and the awareness and experience of natural-self, embodied in the practice of Zen Driving, can be applied to
absolutely everything. Driving is more than a
lyrical analogue of life (''You're just like cross-

town traffic,'' sang Jimi Hendrix), it—Zen Driving, that is—enhances life! Moving Meditation is a very real form of meditation, an authentic practice and expression of Zen Mind. It leads to the realization that the Zen Mind can, truly, be reflected in all that we do and in how we do it. Everything, as Roshi Kapleau says, ''becomes an expression of True-mind, creative and *energizing*.''

EPILOGUE

One day a lonely mendicant named Eikes came across the monastery of the ninety-fifth Patriarch, Hu-sung, and asked if he could borrow his jumper cables. The aging Roshi, an ex-L.A. Bonzai racer, sat in the middle of his grimy garage. He looked at the pitiful Eikes and said, yes, he would give him a free jump if he could answer one question: "What is Zen Driving?"

Eikes's eyes rolled inside his head, he hemmed and hawed, then slowly a smile spread across his face. He said, "Zen Driving is an open mind along an open road."

"Quack!" roared the old Master, and threw a greasy wrench at the lowly monk's head. "Get out'a here and study!"

Eight years later Eikes returned, his battery still dead, looking more bedraggled than before. He asked for another sanzen with the Roshi. The wizened old Master rolled out from beneath his car. He lay there on his back, his ratchet wrench folded across his stomach, and looked up at Eikes. "Well," he said, "what have you to say for yourself?"

Eikes held his head low. "Master," he said. "Please, tell me. What is Zen Driving?"

The Master smiled and said, "Zen Driving is an open mind along an open road." And in that instant Eikes was enlightened! He got his car started.

So now as you sail enjoyably down the highway, you roll down your window and fling this book out into the breeze. After all, what has the juice, the power to transform you into a Zen Driver, lies within yourself. You have your own awareness, you don't need some so-called expert telling you how to drive. You learn from experience. You start from scratch. Every instant! As Shunryu Suzuki says, "In the beginner's mind there are many possibilities, but in the expert's, few." You've decided to become a Zen Driver, and now you are on the road to figuring it out for yourself.

Happy driving!

About the Author

K.T. Berger is brothers Kevin and Todd Berger. Kevin is an editor and free-lance journalist in San Francisco; Todd a practicing psychotherapist.